The Los Angeles
Metropolitan
Experience

THE UNIVERSITY OF
WINCHESTER

Martial Rose Library
Tel: 01962 827306

2 APR 2013

To be returned on or before the day marked above, subject to recall.

Association of American Geographers

Comparative Metropolitan Analysis Project

Vol. 1   Contemporary Metropolitan America: Twenty Geographical Vignettes. Cambridge: Ballinger Publishing Company, 1976.

Vol. 2.   Urban Policymaking and Metropolitan Dynamics: A Comparative Geographical Analysis. Cambridge: Ballinger Publishing Company, 1976.

Vol. 3.   A Comparative Atlas of America's Great Cities: Twenty Metropolitan Regions. Minneapolis: University of Minnesota Press, 1976.

Vignettes of the following metropolitan regions are also published by Ballinger Publishing Company as separate monographs:

- Boston
- New York-New Jersey
- Philadelphia
- Hartford-Central Connecticut
- Baltimore
- New Orleans
- Chicago
- St. Paul-Minneapolis
- Seattle
- Miami
- Los Angeles

Research Director:
John S. Adams, University of Minnesota

Associate Director and Atlas Editor:
Ronald Abler, Pennsylvania State University

Chief Cartographer:
Ki—Suk Lee, University of Minnesota

Steering Committee and Editorial Board:
Brian J.L. Berry, Chairman, University of Chicago
John R. Borchert, University of Minnesota
Frank E. Horton, Southern Illinois University
J. Warren Nystrom, Association of American Geographers
James E. Vance, Jr., University of California, Berkeley
David Ward, University of Wisconsin

Supported by a grant from the National Science Foundation.

The Los Angeles Metropolitan Experience:

Uniqueness, Generality, and the Goal of the Good Life

Howard J. Nelson
and
William A. V. Clark

University of California, Los Angeles

Ballinger Publishing Company ● Cambridge, Massachusetts
A Subsidiary of J.B. Lippincott Company

 This book is printed on recycled paper.

International Standard Book Number: 0-88410-438-9

Library of Congress Catalog Card Number: 76-4795

Printed in the United States of America

Library of Congress Cataloging in Publication Data

Nelson, Howard J
    The Los Angeles metropolitan experience.

    Bibliography: p.
    1. Los Angeles metropolitan area—Social conditions. 2. Los Angeles metropolitan area—Economic conditions. 3. Minorities—Los Angeles metropolitan area. 4. Physical geography—Los Angeles metropolitan area. I. Clark, William A.V., joint author. II. Title.
HN80.L7N44   309.1'794'9405   76-4795
ISBN 0-88410-438-9

Contents

List of Figures

List of Tables

Introduction

Visiting easterners, expatriate Europeans, and newspaper columnists created an image of metropolitan Los Angeles that pictures it as not only different from other cities, but in fact unique. These authors see it as a brand new, rapidly built, sprawling, uncohesive, formless place, totally at variance with traditional patterns of urban settlement. Earlier writings emphasized the singular physical aspects of its site—the juxtaposition of snow-capped mountains, tropical plains, sandy beaches—and its unusual climate—with rainless summers and mild winters. And all the while its residents, often migrants responding to the persistent American dream of California, were developing a lifestyle which emphasized the good life and a break from traditional ways. It is not surprising that the concept of uniqueness has been firmly attached in the popular mind to the Los Angeles metropolis.

Probably no urban region has had more written about it and at the same time less substantive research directed toward an understanding of its form and function than this one. There is a good deal of material related to the physical qualities of its site, the problems involved in its urbanization, and the attempted solution to these problems. Exceptional qualities do appear here. One can also rather easily document its rapid and recent growth in response to technological developments and events of the twentieth century. But in analyzing, in the nineteen seventies, such things as population density, social structure, land use patterns, community identification, journey to work patterns, and similar elements, doubts as to the uniqueness of the metropolis arise. Some recent statistical measures, for example, suggest that Los Angeles is not particularly different from Chicago, Denver, Detroit, Minneapolis, or a host of other American cities.

"LOS ANGELES MAY BE THE ULTIMATE CITY OF OUR AGE ..." —CHRISTOPHER RAND NEW YORKER, OCTOBER 1, 1966

Another group of popular writers, operating from a more contemporary viewpoint, feel that Los Angeles, though different, is not a freak or an aberration, but rather the prototype of the "ultimate city." The feeling that Los Angeles may reflect the city of the future is rooted in several factors. Much of its growth is recent and a large proportion of its built-up area reflects the economic forces, building styles, and cultural notions of the last several decades. For example, almost all of its growth has been during the era of the automobile and most of it during a time when government policy has encouraged the building of single family homes. Then, too, it seems to have been easier for migrants to southern California to break old ties and old habits and to be innovative in a new environment than for those who moved shorter distances to less different locales—

innovation seems to be a characteristic of the area. Developments—or fads—often seem to appear first in California, then spread to the rest of the nation.

It is entirely possible, therefore, that early writers who recognized elements in Los Angeles that they considered unique were simply seeing things that occurred earlier and more recognizably here, but would soon emerge in other metropolitan areas as well. The dynamics of the automobile in the midtwentieth century, for example, an early feature of Los Angeles, now seems to be almost as important in other new and growing portions of metropolitan areas. And the effect of FHA policies in encouraging single family housing and suburban expansion has been nationwide. In this sense, the observers who saw in the Los Angeles of the sixties the direction in which urban America seemed to be headed were reasonably perceptive in their ultimate city connotation.

"LIFE IN LOS ANGELES IS A TONIC." —LOS ANGELES TIMES, 1906

Another pervasive theme of writers on the Los Angeles area over a hundred year period has been an emphasis on the good life possible in this new land. Nordhoff's chapter, "A January Day in Los Angeles," in a book published in 1875, describes the lush winter landscape, with all manner of fruit, vegetables, and flowers available and public and domestic architecture geared to outdoor living. Excursions for weekends to the beaches were common features in the 1880s, and journeys into the mountains were part of the lifestyle dating from about that period. The "California Bungalow" was described as a house style designed to maximize the pleasures of living in a land of gentle climate. Over the years its inhabitants have raised to a high art the goal of the good life. While recent writers have focused on the backyard barbecue, the camper, and the surfboard as symbols of the area, much that is substantial has been done in the area to maintain the quality of urban living for a large and diverse population.

If an important national goal is to improve the quality of life for all Americans, and today most Americans are urban Americans, then it may be particularly appropriate to examine the experience of urban Los Angeles in its attempt to solve problems affecting the quality of life of its residents. Many problems facing urban America may not be solvable in any final way; rather, there will be a variety of attempts over time to produce solutions which, in fact, will prove to be transitory. An examination of the Los Angeles experience is important for two reasons: the area compressed the population growth and spatial expansion of the older metropolitan areas into a much shorter time span, and the quality of urban life has from the first been one of the major assets of the area. Therefore, it is not surprising that the city pioneered and innovated in producing and implementing solutions to situations which threatened the efficiency and amenity of urban life, qualities that its citizens particularly cherished.

This study then will have three major aims. First, it inquires to what extent the Los Angeles area is unique today and to what extent it is similar to other American metropolitan areas. Second, it examines the prediction that Los Angeles is the ultimate city and that its characteristics forecast the direction that will be taken by other cities in their growth and arrangement. Finally, it illustrates that, in its search for the good life, the Los Angeles area has had to find early solutions to urban problems that are becoming general. What can be extracted from the Los Angeles metropolitan experience that is useful to metropolitan areas in general?

THE EXTENT OF THE REGION

Los Angeles is the urban focus of an eleven county region unusual in its areal extent, numbers of people, recency of growth, and in its topographical, climatic, and economic diversity (Figure 1). Long isolated at the far corner of the country, its economic capacities were predominantly agricultural until World War II. Since 1940 it has been transformed by a vast population migration into a region where the central city has assumed metropolitan characteristics very similar to other large cities and both the agricultural activities and the wild landscapes of the hinterland have become increasingly urban oriented. The region is unusually extensive. Its 58,700 square miles are comparable in area to a state the size of New York or Michigan, while its Pacific shoreline extends for 435 miles, from Morro Bay to the Mexican border.

Figure 1. The eleven county metropolitan region and Los Angeles daily urban system.

However, topographical features, climatic conditions, and the lack of agricultural or industrial development minimize the economic importance of much of the vast region. Perhaps half of the total area is in rugged mountains and is either sparsely settled or empty of people. Another large portion of the region to the east is desert or semidesert, largely uninhabited save for the occasional homesteader, and generally left to cactus and the jackrabbit. Reflecting its uneconomical nature, nearly half of the entire region is in public ownership—national forests, military reservations, Indian land, and the like (Figure 2).

The Los Angeles region, therefore, does not have quite the relationship to its urban center as other metropolitan situations around the country. The mountains are much used recreational areas both summer and winter, close enough for weekend use. Large areas of the desert, too, serve a recreational purpose for activities as varied as those of the "rock hound" and the dune buggy fanatic. Beyond that, this area is familiar to the Angeleno mainly as a route of passage—to the Sierras, Las Vegas, Arizona, or points "back East."

These generalizations should not be taken to imply that the Los Angeles hinterland is uniformly without development. The Coachella and Imperial valleys have been transformed by irrigation into two of California's most productive agricultural areas. Palm Springs

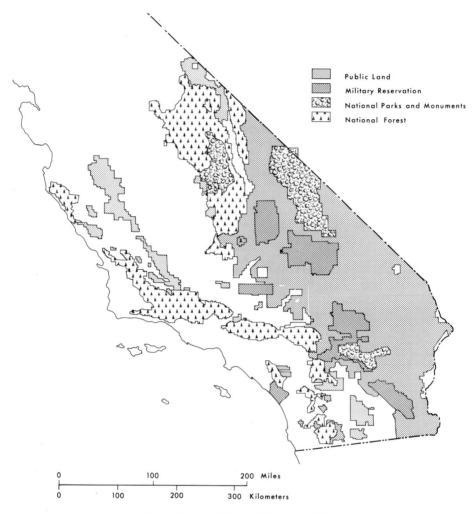

Public Land

Military Reservation

National Parks and Monuments

National Forest

| 0 | 100 | 200 Miles |
| 0 | 100 | 200 | 300 Kilometers |

Figure 2.   Land in public ownership.

(and its satellites), on the edge of the desert, is a booming winter resort of both regional and national importance. To the north in the Antelope Valley are the nascent cities of Lancaster and Palmdale, awaiting further aerospace spillover into their sunny desert locations. And near the latter community twenty-seven square miles are being purchased for a proposed Palmdale Intercontinental Airport. Only a small fraction of the region consists of coastal plains and their connecting valleys, the scene of intensive irrigated agriculture (mainly citrus) early in this century and today the location of almost all of the people in the region.

The immediate Los Angeles metropolis is the home of nearly ten million persons. One hundred and fifty miles to the south, San Diego, with its superb natural harbor, has grown to a metropolis of 1.4 million people, based on a growing aerospace industry, military installations (headquarters for the Sixth Fleet), and resort and retirement activity. A hundred miles to the north, Santa Barbara has developed from a retirement community for the wealthy into a regional center of 250,000 persons. And along the same coast, Ventura and Oxnard, sleepy agricultural villages thirty years ago, have similar sized populations and are rapidly expanding onto the agricultural land that first supported them.

The existence of population clusters of this order of magnitude is a remarkably recent

Table 1. Employment Structures for Selected Metropolitan Areas

Percent Employment in:	Boston	Chicago	Cleveland	Dallas	Denver	Detroit	Los Angeles	Minneapolis-St. Paul	New York	Philadelphia	Pittsburgh	San Francisco-Oakland	Seattle-Everett	St. Louis
Agriculture, Forestry, and Fisheries	0.5	0.6	0.7	1.3	1.3	0.5	1.0	0.7	0.4	0.5	0.7	1.1	1.3	1.1
Mining	0.06	0.1	0.2	1.0	1.2	0.1	0.3	0.08	0.1	0.08	0.9	0.2	0.1	0.3
Construction	5.0	4.8	4.6	6.7	6.2	4.3	4.5	5.4	4.3	5.1	5.3	5.4	5.7	5.0
Manufacturing	22.4	31.7	35.4	23.4	17.0	37.4	27.3	24.7	20.7	29.7	31.7	16.7	24.2	28.8
Transportation	3.3	5.0	3.5	4.4	4.6	2.9	3.5	4.9	5.3	3.5	4.2	6.0	5.0	4.7
Communications	1.9	1.4	1.6	1.5	1.8	1.3	1.8	1.3	2.1	1.3	1.2	2.1	1.8	1.4
Utilities and Sanitary Services	1.5	1.6	1.5	1.7	1.6	1.4	1.5	1.3	1.9	1.7	1.7	2.0	1.4	1.7
Wholesale Trade	4.8	4.8	4.7	6.4	5.8	4.2	4.8	6.3	5.0	4.4	4.0	5.1	5.8	5.4
Retail	16.2	16.0	14.9	16.7	17.0	15.7	15.9	16.7	14.9	16.1	16.4	15.7	16.1	15.8
Banking-Insurance	7.5	6.0	4.8	8.1	6.6	4.7	6.3	6.3	9.5	6.0	4.5	8.0	6.9	5.1
Bus and Repair Service	3.6	3.9	3.4	4.3	4.0	3.1	4.9	4.4	5.0	3.5	3.3	4.6	3.3	2.9
Personal Services	2.7	2.9	2.6	3.7	3.4	2.6	3.0	2.7	3.1	2.8	2.7	3.3	2.9	3.1
Entertainment and Recreation	0.7	0.7	0.7	0.9	1.0	0.7	1.9	0.9	1.3	0.6	0.8	1.1	1.0	0.8
Hospitals and Health Services	7.7	4.7	5.5	4.3	6.9	5.7	5.6	6.7	6.0	5.8	6.2	6.3	5.7	5.7
Schools and Colleges	9.6	6.7	6.6	6.3	9.2	6.7	6.9	8.3	7.3	6.9	7.4	8.1	8.8	7.3
Professional Services (legal, engineering)	4.4	3.0	2.7	2.8	3.2	2.5	3.2	2.7	4.3	3.2	2.5	4.1	2.8	2.5
Public Administration	5.9	4.4	4.3	3.6	6.6	4.1	4.7	4.1	5.7	6.2	4.1	7.3	4.7	5.6
Other	2.4	2.0	2.2	2.9	2.6	2.2	2.7	2.6	3.1	2.6	2.6	3.2	2.6	2.8

Source: U.S. Bureau of the Census, Census of Population 1970, General Social and Economic Characteristics by State.

phenomenon. At the turn of the century the population of the city of Los Angeles was only 102,000 (compared to 3.5 million in New York at that time). All of southern California contained only 325,000 persons. However, by 1940 there were ten times that many—3.7 million. Since that date the population has increased to almost twelve million. No state, save for California itself, experienced a larger total population increase over the thirty year period. The region now has nearly one-third of the population of the thirteen western states.

Although a portion of this population resulted from natural increase, much of it was through migration. Since 1940 about five million persons have migrated to southern California, perhaps the most extensive movement of population to a small area within a short time span that the country has ever seen. Americans migrated to the region for jobs in aircraft plants and shipyards during World War II, to work in the war industry at the time of the Korean conflict, and to help in the development of the country's missile-space capability in the later 1950s. But they also came in droves, as they had all along, in search of the good life in an area of climatic permissiveness, topographic interest, and a glamorous reputation. No wonder Frank Lloyd Wright exclaimed, "It is as if you tipped the United States up so all the commonplace people slid down into Southern California" (*Los Angeles Times,* January 20, 1940).

Major changes in the economy have accompanied the massive increase in population. Specialized agriculture and tourism are no longer such important components of the economy. Manufacturing employment (as is usual in urban centers) is now the single largest employment category. However, many of the specialized activities of the region were established in the first three decades of the century, early in the city's existence. Petroleum became important in the twenties and during the same period the area became the world center of motion picture production—attracted by the area's varied scenery and bright sunshine essential for early outdoor film making. An incipient aircraft manufacturing industry developed in

the 1920s. It was the aircraft industry that brought vast expansion in industrial employment during World War II and provided an important base for postwar growth as well. Industrial employment doubled in the decade of the 1950s, increasing at twice the rate of the population growth. For example, from 1958 to 1968 the Long Beach-Los Angeles SMSA added 556,000 nonagricultural workers to its payrolls, the largest numerical gain of any SMSA in the nation. As a result, the proportions of workers in the various industrial categories today, are about average for large American metropolitan centers (Table 1).

With the expansion of population, the landscape near the urban centers has been transformed. The rural scenes typical of the coastal valleys—orange groves, walnut orchards, vineyards, fields of winter vegetables, and large expanses of barley—have been replaced by subdivisions of tract houses, shopping centers, and freeways. Citrus, the area's most important crop in the 1940s, now accounts for only about 15 percent of the total agricultural production. The dairy industry, once highly developed in its dry-lot form in the Artesia area, has moved into Riverside County and the San Joaquin Valley. Some vegetables, once produced locally, are now imported from Mexico.

Significantly, much market-oriented agriculture has survived urban growth and flourishes on it. The area is the nation's leader in the production of nursery stock and cut flowers. Riverside County produces more eggs than any other of the nation's counties. Also located within the region are areas important for specialty vegetables such as broccoli, lima beans, spinach, cantaloupe, and watermelon, and such tree crops as oranges, lemons, and avocados are produced and marketed locally. Yet total agricultural production in the area had a gross value of $1.3 billion in 1968, up 20 percent in the decade despite massive losses of land to the subdivider. Nevertheless, the agricultural ring has been pushed inexorably back by the urban frontier; no farming activity is immune and the demand for urban space will likely continue this trend.

The Physical Setting and Natural Hazards

"Life in a land of sunshine" described the Los Angeles metropolis in the eyes of an essayist fifty years ago. Christmas cards featuring blooming orange trees set against a snow-covered mountain backdrop were sent by residents to their friends back East as late as the 1940s. The surfer on a curling wave, or a sun-tanned bikini clad beach girl still illustrate popular articles on southern California. But the natural landscape can be the source of other images. National attention focused on the Bel Air fire in 1961 and the winter floods of that same year. The Palisades landslides of 1958 and the San Fernando earthquake of 1971 were other natural disasters, and the area's air pollution has introduced "smog" into the country's vocabulary.

In southern California, perhaps more than for any other urban region in America, the natural environment was to be and still is a prime element in the "good life" of its inhabitants. The major item was the rarest of all climates, characterized by warm winters and rainless summers. Included also were the miles of sandy beaches, the looming mountain backdrop, and the lush green connecting valleys. The importance of the natural environment to the life of the resident of the Los Angeles metropolis cannot be underestimated, and has been used as an organizing theme by many commentators on the Los Angeles scene.

THE INTERCONNECTIONS OF TOPOGRAPHIES: SEASHORE, PLAIN, HILL, AND MOUNTAIN

Southern California comprises a high, rugged mountain border; low but precipitous intervening hills; broad, flat valley bottoms; low-lying coastal plains; and skirting sandy beaches (Figure 3). This spacious and varied site provides the physical locale for a great variety of homesites, work places, and recreational activities that add much to the satisfaction of the inhabitants.

The high mountain wall that bounds the region extends eastward from Point Conception to Cajon Pass (the Transverse ranges) and then south-southeast into Mexico (The Peninsula ranges). Behind Los Angeles they are known as the Santa Susanas, the San Gabriels, and the San Bernardinos, respectively. A name popular with an older generation was, appropriately, the Sierra Madre, for eons ago it was the material from these heights that filled the valleys and built the plains. Today these mountains shield the metropolis from continental storms and catch the rainfall that helps water the area. Between the high mountains and the sea, lower but still rugged ranges—the Santa Monicas, the Verdugos, the Santa Anas—extend like fingers, dividing the lowlands into a number of distinctive parts. The San Fernando, San Gabriel,

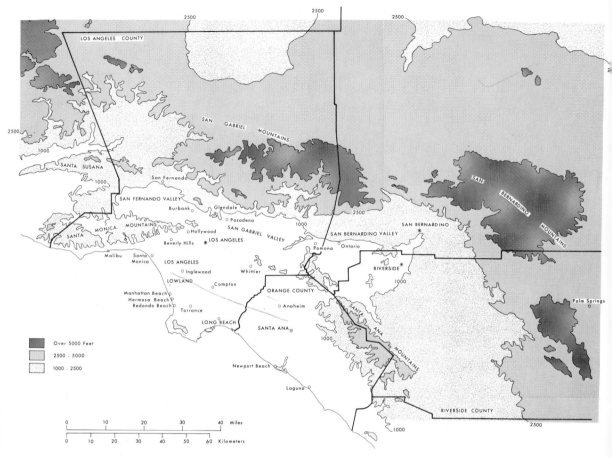

Figure 3. Topography.

and San Bernardino valleys are inland. Seaward of these ranges is the extensive Los Angeles lowland. In the southwest corner of this lowland is the promontory of Palos Verdes Hills.

The pronounced variation in topography within this single urban area must be experienced to be appreciated. As Jonathan Garst puts it, "Nothing can be more striking than the change from the steep, eroded slopes of the mountains to the flat, smooth, alluvial floors of the filled valleys. There are, in reality, no foothills ... one steps from plain to mountain." For Reyner Banham the mountain "fingers" provide a distinctive subregion or "ecology," and a wider focus brings the higher mountain wall into the same scene. Lines of desirable foothill communities have developed along their margins, including Hollywood, West Hollywood, Beverly Hills, Bel Air, Brentwood, and Pacific Palisades along the south slopes of

the Santa Monicas. However, similar strings of communities have developed along a half dozen other mountain ranges. This "foothill ecology" is characterized as having "narrow, tortuous residential roads serving precipitous house plots that often back up directly on unimproved wilderness even now," or conversely, "an air of deeply buried privacy even in relatively broad valley-bottoms in Stone Canyon or Mandeville Canyon...." Here high-class homesites are available for those who wish to enjoy spectacular views from the hillsides, or the seclusion of their "laurel privacies" in the canyons.

The mountain wall is generally too precipitous for homesites save at the very base of the slopes and the crest lines of the San Gabriels are sharp and uninhabited. But more level areas are available on the higher San Bernardino Mountains. Here, resort communities developed early around mountain lakes formed where valleys have been dammed as reservoirs for irrigation projects. Bear Valley was dammed in 1884 forming Big Bear Lake; Lake Arrowhead was a later undertaking. Today they have been transformed into mountaintop resort-suburbs among the pines with elevations of about 5,100 feet to 6,700 respectively, but are still accessible to downtown Los Angeles by a ninety minute drive.

The mountains have been part of the southern California lifestyle for at least a century. An observatory on Mount Wilson was reached by toll road, and an inclined railway up neighboring Echo Mountain (with resort hotels at both top and bottom) stimulated interest in the ranges behind Pasadena as a recreational area accessible by interurban rail line in the 1880s. Acquired by the government as forest reserve in the 1890s, the area has seen rapidly increasing use for hiking, fishing, camping, weekend cabins, and occasional skiing, all within the metropolitan area. Romantically named roads —"Angeles Crest Highway," "Rim of the World Drive," and the "Pines to Palms Highway"— provide access to the mountains for weekend excursions or Sunday drives.

The three interior valleys of San Fernando, San Gabriel, and San Bernardino, and the coastal plain, comprise Banham's "Plains of Id," a second distinctive "ecology" and lifestyle for the area's residents. These flatlands provide the world with its stereotyped image of Los Angeles: "An endless plain endlessly gridded with endless streets, peppered endlessly with ticky-tacky houses clustered in indistinguishable neighborhoods." But in fact, careful observation reveals considerable neighborhood variety. The age of a neighborhood is often reflected in its architecture, and blocks of "California Bungalows" built just prior to World War I are not easily confused with areas of white stucco and red tiled "Spanish Colonial" homes of the twenties or with sections of post–World War II ranch style houses (Figure 4). Again, previous agricultural occupance is occasionally reflected in common dooryard trees, with areas earlier devoted to English walnuts, oranges, or olives still identifiable.

But there is a more significant aspect of the Plains of Id for "this is where Los Angeles is most like other cities: Anywheresville/Nowheresville ... the only parts of Los Angeles flat enough and boring enough to compare with cities of the Middle West." A resident of the plains, however, might point to the bordering mountains visible in many directions, which not only add interest to the horizon, but also provide useful orientation to daily movement. But the flatness has served the metropolis well, for it was across these flat plains that the early interurban lines could run, bringing the city to the beaches and into the mountains.

The separation of the valleys and coastal plains by the mountain ranges produces climatic variations between the several lowlands that encourage distinctive ways of life among superficially similar neighborhoods. Although subtle to the observer, these differences in daily weather are of major importance to the life of the residents and are a significant factor in the choice of a residential location (Figure 5). For example, the resident of a townhouse in Inglewood (a community near the international airport) on the Los Angeles coastal plain experiences a distinctly marine climate. This climatic area extends inland about as far as the Los Angeles City Hall, and southward to Santa Ana. On the other hand, the owner of a single family house in the western San Fernando Valley community of Canoga Park lives in a more continental climate, generally typical of the inland valleys. Although the distance from one of these communities to the other is only about twenty-five miles, their encounters with southern California climates are markedly different, and serve nicely to illustrate local variations in daily weather on the Plains of Id.

A July day in Inglewood may begin with the sky overcast or even foggy and with the humidity about 60 percent. The sun may "burn through" late in the morning, with the temperature reaching a maximum of about 75 degrees, although the sensible temperature seems lower due to a brisk breeze sweeping in from the ocean. High clouds and a temperature of 65 or so come with the evening. Winter night temperatures, on the other hand, are the highest in the area, averaging nearly 50 degrees in January. Afternoon temperatures in that same month average about 65 degrees. Bougainvillea, Burmese honeysuckle, and cup-of-gold vine climb arbor and house; cherimoya and other tropical fruits grace an occasional backyard.

The same July day in Canoga Park may dawn bright and clear, with the temperature heading for a maximum reading of about 95 degrees. However, the humidity is low and the noon temperature is not uncomfortable in the

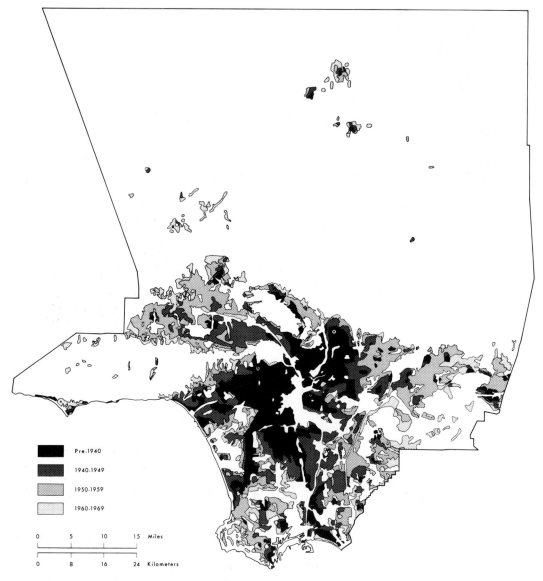

Figure 4. Age of housing.

shade, although the sun is hot. The evenings remain warm, but the night temperature of the clear air may fall to nearly 60 degrees. Swimming pools abound in valley yards, and air conditioning is common in both home and car. Winter days also tend to be sunny with January maximums of nearly 70 degrees, although the nights are quite cold with minimums of about 40 degrees. Frost occurs on about ten nights in winter. The combination of warm summers and mild winters with much sunshine in all seasons is probably the closest to the nation's image of the southern California climate.

Thus the resident of Inglewood might need a sweater or jacket to be comfortable on the same July day that the Canoga Park citizen would find a dip in the pool a relief from the heat of the afternoon. The balmy evenings, however, make the inland location the home of the backyard barbecue while the maritime dweller may find his dining room more com-

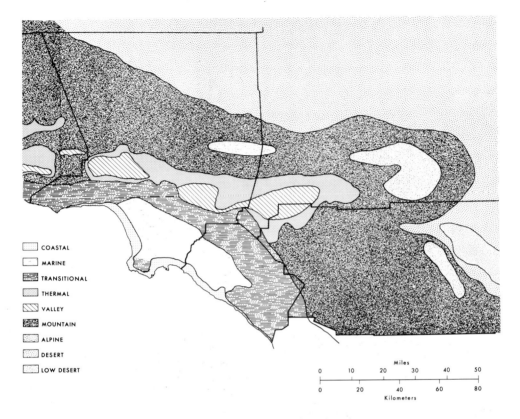

Figure 5. Climatic zones in the Los Angeles area.

fortable than the chill of the night air. In January, however, cars parked in the open overnight in the valleys will be covered with frost in the morning (which the owner will wash off with his omnipresent garden hose), while the coastal automobile under the same conditions will have only a layer of dew.

A third and final topographical division is the immediate coastal strip of beach and adjacent residences that runs some seventy miles from Malibu to Balboa and encompasses the beach cities of Santa Monica, Playa del Rey, Venice, Manhattan Beach, Hermosa Beach, Redondo Beach, Long Beach, Huntington Beach, and Newport. This subregion—"Surf-urbia" to Banham—makes the Los Angeles metropolis "the greatest city-on-the-shore in the world." The miles of white sand beach, most of it accessible to the public, the numerous piers extending into the sea, and the yacht harbors such as Marina del Rey, San Pedro, Newport, and Laguna provide a singular beach culture with its own artifacts (the surfboard), and an ideal *locale* for the cultivation and cult

of the physical man and woman. Angelenos started the then long trek to the beach for outings in the 1870s and came in droves in later decades when many of the beach cities were developed at the ends of the interurban railroads.

But even the beach has been affected by urban growth and change. Beaches formerly in equilibrium (between sand removed and sand supplied by wave action) have suffered from the erection of structures on sand dune areas and on areas of sand-producing rock, and through the building of dams. Construction of jetties and breakwaters interrupted the movement of sand along the shore. As a result, a number of recreational beaches have been stripped away and remain only through artificial replenishment of sand. A long term solution awaits ecological planning over wider units and on a larger scale than has yet been achieved.

Additionally, the liquid wastes of ten million urban dwellers are disposed of at sea, with outfall sewers discharging five and seven miles offshore. Since the installation of more advanced processing devices in 1950 the beaches have been largely pollution free. Constant vigilance is essential, however, and in compliance with the Regional Water Quality Control Board's monitoring program, seventeen testing stations in Santa Monica Bay sample the water daily.

PROBLEMS OF THE SITE

Although the natural environment of Los Angeles provides a particularly fruitful scene for the achievement of a quality urban life with variety and openness, it also presents problems unusual in their magnitude and diversity. Significant topographic, hydrologic, and atmospheric problems have existed throughout the development of the metropolis. At first there was the problem of an adequate supply of water and now there is air pollution, which strikes at the heart of the pleasant climate throughout the region. Earthquakes also menace the entire area, although other natural problems present a more localized threat to California living. Winter floods concern mainly the residents of the lowlands, while autumn fires or sudden landslides worry the dwellers of mountain slope or canyon.

Water and Floods

An adequate and reliable supply of water is essential to any life and is particularly important for a metropolitan region. The founding padres located their urban nucleus at a point on the then perennial Los Angeles River where water could be most easily obtained for irrigation. Significantly, the Civic Center of today's city has not migrated far from the original inland spot. But even with the Los Angeles River, the early settlement was dry and dusty. B.F. Taylor visited the area in 1879 and described the scene: "Tree and shrub, except where transfigured with the witchery of water, are powdery as a miller's coat, and the dry fields are thickly strewn with 'Graham flour'. . . . Palm leaves are as gray as an elephant's ears, and portions of the landscape have a disused air." Only a few crops could be grown without irrigation. Urban expansion and the creation of a lush landscape depended on the "witchery of water." The Los Angeles River was tapped, of course, winter runoff was salvaged, and artesian supplies were soon dis-

covered. However, it was clear that population increase would be severely limited without important water.

In 1905 the city of Los Angeles passed two bond issues by majorities of fourteen to one and ten to one to finance the importation of water from the Owens Valley, on the east side of the Sierra Nevada 225 miles to the north. As a result, the city of Los Angeles possessed more water than it could immediately use and decided to offer water to neighboring cities if they were willing to be annexed. It was this decision that has largely determined the areal characteristics of the present city. Within fifteen years, fifty-nine separate annexations increased the size of Los Angeles from 107 to over 440 square miles, absorbing ten previously independent cities as well as the agricultural San Fernando Valley. As a result, Los Angeles became for many years the country's largest city (in terms of area). Vast tracts of land have been available for subdivision within the city limits down to the present decade, enabling this "central city" to gain population annually while others were losing population to their suburbs.

By the 1920s many of the remaining suburban communities, originally sited at spots where small amounts of water would be obtained by damming mountain canyons or tapping artesian aquifers, were facing water shortages. With impetus from Los Angeles in 1924 a claim was filed on a flow of 1,500 cubic feet of water per second from the Colorado River. The Metropolitan Water District—a state-created entity, with taxing power, designed to be a wholesaler of water—was formed and soon constructed the largest and longest domestic water supply line in the United States. While only eleven cities comprised the original district, today it includes 122 incorporated cities and much unincorporated area. The 4,800 square miles within its borders include almost all of the populated parts of coastal southern California from Santa Barbara to San Diego (Figure 6).

A state water project was authorized by the voters of California in 1960. The project includes a 450 mile California aqueduct that will ultimately bring over two million acre feet of water from northern to southern California and will compensate for presumed reduced supplies from the Colorado pursuant to a Supreme Court decision in 1964. Perhaps it is because of

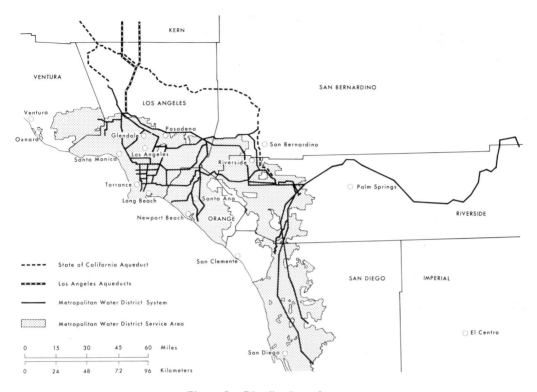

KERN

VENTURA

SAN BERNARDINO

LOS ANGELES

Ventura

Oxnard

Pasadena

Glendale

Los Angeles

San Bernardino

Santa Monica

Riverside

Torrance

Palm Springs

Long Beach

Santa Ana

RIVERSIDE

Newport Beach

ORANGE

San Clemente

San Diego

IMPERIAL

- - - - - State of California Aqueduct

▪▪▪▪▪ Los Angeles Aqueducts

——— Metropolitan Water District System

Metropolitan Water District Service Area

El Centro

0   15   30   45   60 Miles

0   24   48   72   96 Kilometers

San Diego

Figure 6. Distribution of water.

an awareness of the area's need that both water management and conservation are highly developed. Rainfall is retained in reservoirs or goes into natural underground basins from which it can be pumped—only a small percentage escapes into the ocean. Water Replenishment Districts have been formed and have authority to levy assessments for ground water extraction and use and to purchase water for maintaining ground water basins.

With the growth of the urban population, a large proportion of water eventually ends up in the sewer system. Today, three major sewage collection systems discharge (after treatment) copious quantities into the ocean, with the Los Angeles County area alone contributing some 700 million gallons a day. The possibility that a portion of this waste water can be reclaimed is good. Sewage reclamation plants were established as early as 1926. The Los Angeles County Sanitation District has operated a reclamation plant in the Whittier Narrows since 1962, and currently 18,000 acre feet of treated water annually are sold to the Central and West Basin Replenishment Districts

for aquifer recharge. Additional plants are under construction.

Today only the wild landscape (still clearly visible on hillside and mountain slope) has an arid look. The planted landscape is lush and green the year around, reflecting a fertile soil, long frost-free season, and universal irrigation. Water is physically plentiful, the rates are low, and metropolitan Los Angeles has not endured a water shortage within memory. It is used extravagantly, even for such things as washing down driveways and sweeping fallen leaves from the manicured lawns. (The westerner, incidentally, is constantly surprised at what he considers to be the generally unkept look of the lawn in the parts of the country where the grass grows naturally).

To the average citizen the water problem of southern California seems to have been solved reasonably well. It has been relatively easy to marshall public support in the area for financing water supply facilities well in advance of critical shortages, perhaps because it was an obvious and universally understood need. Forgotten are the frustrations of the Owens Valley residents who saw water from their area exported to a distant city. Almost unnoticed are the real estate taxes levied by the Metropolitan Water District to make possible its low water rates. Kept in the background is the controversy over the California Water Plan, reflecting increased ecological concern and the potential adverse effect water diversion could have on San Francisco Bay. And in the future loom the high repayment costs to be levied on the urban users of water from that system. What is clear is that the local and regional solutions possible in the past have now been shifted to the state and national levels and assent of these larger constituencies may be necessary for any increased water needs in the future.

Coping with floods, to make the plains safely habitable in a region noted for an occasional deluge, has proved more difficult. In southern California torrential downpours sometimes occur when the ground is already saturated with earlier winter precipitation, and dangerous flash floods and mud flows can easily follow.

Many of the valley floors are natural settling basins, and much of the Los Angeles coastal lowland is an extensive flood plain (Figure 7). These plains where floodwaters once ran unconfined are now the location of all the complex structures of a modern urban area. In an attempt to protect the city, federal and local agencies have introduced a wide variety of flood control devices (Figure 8).

The beginning of organized flood control in southern California dates from 1914, when the County Flood Control District was organized in response to a catastrophic flood of that year. Federal help came after 1936 when the United States Army Corps of Engineers was given authority and funds for work on the major streams flowing through the city. At the same time the Department of Agriculture assumed responsibility for the headwaters and small tributaries. Vegetation has been planted to discourage runoff, check dams have been constructed, and storage reservoirs have been built. Channels have been straightened and

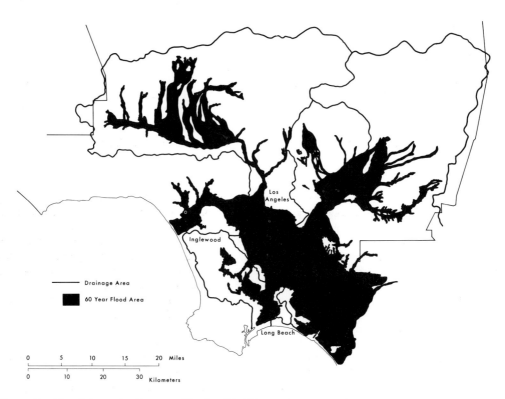

Figure 7. Flood hazards. Source: Charles W. Eliot and Donald F. Griffin, *Waterlines . . . Key to Development of Metropolitan Los Angeles* (Los Angeles: Haynes Foundation, 1946), pp. 12–13.

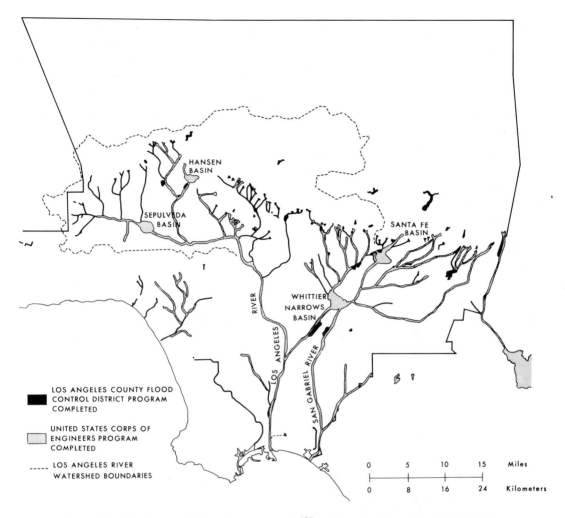

Figure 8. Flood control. Data Source: Los Angeles County Flood Control District.

paved, several low areas have been zoned to prohibit structures, and both public builders and private subdividers have been warned of areas subject to flood. The state real estate commissioner requires every subdivider to show a flood danger report to a prospective home buyer. The cost of this extensive program totals several billion dollars since 1938.

Yet success remains elusive. In January 1969 several storms produced a major flood in which ninety-two persons died and 10,000 were driven from their homes. Physical damage was estimated at $62 million, most of which occurred in areas of recent urban growth where control plans and facilities had not kept pace with extended urbanization. One engineer quot-

ed by Rantz described the problem as being "well-nigh imposs:ble of complete solution on the one hand and a necessity on the other." However, the fear of flood does not seriously reduce the enjoyment of the good life by the Angeleno. The hazard is only occasional and is then highly localized and the risk of reoccurrence soon fades from the memory of even those previously involved.

Wind and Fire

Wildfire in the brush similarly affects only a miniscule portion of the homes in the metropolis, and in relatively few areas, although the smoke plume that a fire generates may blacken the sky over much of the urban area. Urban fire hazard is the result of the partial urbanization of the rugged Santa Monica Mountains and other ranges that are now part of the metropolitan site. Houses are strung like ribbons into these ranges, following streets in canyon bottoms or on the ridge lines. To reduce erosion, lower costs, and retain the natural feeling of the setting, the slopes between canyons are left in brush. This intimate juxtaposition of brush and residence in hilly terrain sets the scene for disaster.

The brush, known from its major botanical element as chaparral, is highly flammable under certain conditions. These conditions are provided annually in the autumn by the Santa Ana winds, which both dry out the vegetation, increasing its flammability, and provide the draft that speeds the flames across the hills. Most fires are put out promptly by a wary and experienced fire department. However, during the fifteen year period between 1950 and 1965,

243 fires, each involving over one hundred acres, burned over 332,000 acres in Los Angeles and Ventura counties alone (Figure 9). And between November 6 and 8, 1961, the Bel Air-Brentwood conflagration became the costliest fire disaster in California since the San Francisco earthquake and fire of 1906. A three year drought had made the brush tinder dry. Very low humidity and high Santa Ana winds multiplied the fire hazard. The fire, originating in a pile of brush trimmings, spread with unbelievable speed across brush-covered canyons and ridges occupied mainly by high value single family dwellings, most with wood shingle or shake roofs. There was no loss of life, but the insured property loss was about $24 million. Again, in September 1970 a combination of temperatures in the 90s, humidity of 4 percent, and strong Santa Ana winds resulted in fourteen major fires, with the fire line extending from Newhall to Malibu, a distance of

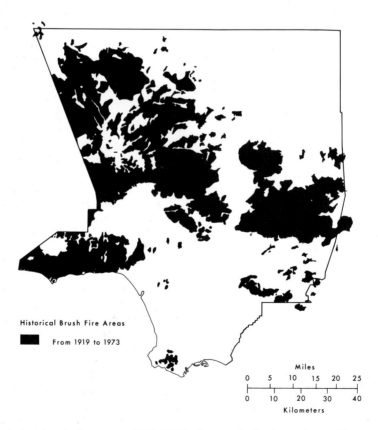

Historical Brush Fire Areas

From 1919 to 1973

Miles
0   5   10   15   20   25

0   10   20   30   40
Kilometers

Figure 9. Historical brush fire areas, 1919–1973. Source: Preliminary Safety Element, Los Angeles County Regional Planning Commission.

thirty-five miles. Three persons died, 295 homes were destroyed, and 180,000 acres of brush were burned. Studies over time indicate the incidence of fire is increasing, presumably due to the burgeoning population and the consequent enhanced opportunity for man-originated fire, both accidental and on purpose.

The ultimate solution to these brush-fed city wildfires is probably the complete urbanization of the mountains and the consequent removal of the brush. In the interim, restrictions on the use of wooden shingles, removal of brush from close proximity of dwellings, and an alert and competent fire department are preventive measures. The substitution of fire retardant vegetation for the extremely flammable chaparral may be an interim expedient.

Slips, Slumps, and Earthquakes

While the "everlasting hills" of a religious song is not a useful description of a region plagued by earthquakes, at the same time southern California and Los Angeles are not likely to break off and fall into the ocean. Landslides in the hills and cliffs are the concern of a few, but earthquake temblors can affect the entire region.

Both the low mountain ranges of the region and the sea cliffs that border it offer possibilities for home sites with truly spectacular views. So the tops of the hills have been leveled, building pads have been scraped out of their sides, and in some instances homes have been extended out on stilts or cantilevers over the slopes. Occasionally, however, the selection of these choice spots for building can lead to personal disaster, for hills and sea cliffs with precipitous slopes tend to be unstable, particularly when saturated by winter rains or following manmade changes in the drainage pattern. A few slumps and slides occur every wet winter, often affecting homes that have appeared stable for a decade or more and occasionally damaging residences in the canyon below. Sometimes the slides are extensive, as at Portuguese Bend, where mass movement affected some 300 acres and destroyed 150 houses. But normally slides are small, each involving only a few houses, more of a nagging worry to the hill homeowner than a realized danger to the city at large.

Much public effort has gone into the formulation of grading ordinances designed to identify unstable slopes and to prevent future slides. Current knowledge and procedures have done much to reduce risk for newly constructed homes. But many older situations are uncorrected and uncorrectable. The region is reputed to be the home of more engineering geologists than any other metropolis—and with good reason.

Another localized hazard is subsidence. Subsidence resulting from the removal of petroleum from underground strata is reported to have been involved in the failure of the Baldwin Hills Reservoir in 1963. As the result of an earthcrack, perhaps associated with tectonic activities as well as petroleum withdrawal, the Baldwin Hills Reservoir failed. Five lives were lost, scores of homes were destroyed, and property damage totaled $62 million. However, the world record for subsidence, approximately thirty feet, occurred in the Wilmington oil field. The area that subsided over this coastal field was intensively industrialized and initially was only from five to ten feet above sea level. The area was soon well below sea level, and much diking and raising of dock facilities was required. Further surface deformation caused extensive damage to pipelines, railroad tracks, and buildings. Subsidence was halted in 1966 by repressurization in conjunction with the recovery of oil.

The southern California metropolis is located in one of the most geologically active regions in the country. Faults crisscross the area (Figure 10). From time to time temblors occur, and as the area has been increasingly occupied, they damage structures and take lives. While only an occasional hazard, the precise region that will be subjected to shake damage is unpredictable and the entire area is earthquake prone. In general, structures built on material that is well consolidated (the mountainous areas) are apt to sustain less damage than those on the alluvial floors of the valleys, and in the valleys the risk is related to the nature and depth of the alluvium.

But the real defense against earthquake damage is to build structures that are resistant to the horizontal forces induced by ground shaking. Generally building codes of both the counties and cities were revised after the Long Beach Earthquake of 1933, in which 120 persons lost their lives. Many public buildings, especially schools, were condemned, torn down, and replaced. The Los Angeles Depart-

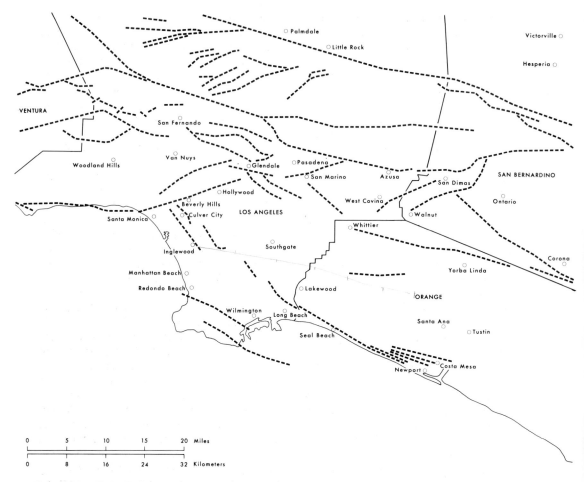

Figure 10. Fault lines. Source: County of Los Angeles Earthquake Commission, Report of the Los Angeles County Earthquake Commission, *San Fernando Earthquake*, 9 February 1971, p. 7.

ment of Building Safety is one of the few such agencies in the nation to require a structural engineering review of all building plans. Yet in spite of a high consciousness of potential earthquake damage, few residents carry earthquake insurance on their dwellings.

Structures again were tested by the San Fernando Earthquake of 1971. Although sixty-four persons died, and damage reached $553 million, the typical wood-frame and stucco house came through reasonably well. The death toll was high at a veterans' hospital near the epicenter of the quake and in several multiple family pre-1933 structures. Tall buildings, new to the area, although built to the best engineering standards of the day, are a question mark in any future serious quake.

Sun and Smog

Year round sunshine, warm temperatures, and light winds have been among southern California's most attractive climatic features and the basis of her renowned outdoor living. However, these same climatic elements combine to produce atmospheric conditions poorly suited to receive the wastes of urbanized man. Low level thermal inversions, which restrict vertical diffusion of pollutants, and the blocking effect of the surrounding mountains act together to reduce drastically the dilution capacity of the local atmosphere. The bright and generally present sunshine is the energizer in the reaction that transforms gaseous wastes into eye-irritating, vegetation-damaging, visibility reducing, health hazardous haze—photochemical smog.

But smog is no longer unique to Los Angeles, and southern California has pioneered more than most areas in attempting to reduce atmospheric pollution since it became a problem here in the early 1940s. The Los Angeles County Air Pollution Control District, a state body, was formed in 1947. The officers are the county supervisors. The district contains seventy-six cities, seven million people, and an area half the size of Massachusetts. Its regulations affect every inhabitant. Open refuse burning is forbidden and in 1957 one and a half million home incinerators were closed. Industrial sources of pollution are controlled by a permit system that requires the installation of control devices. Steam electric generating plants have been required to burn only natural gas or low sulfur oil. However, more than 80 percent of the 14,500 tons of pollutants still fed into the air of Los Angeles County come from some four million vehicles that burn eight million gallons of gasoline a day. Despite regulations on the amount of olefins that may be present in gasoline sold in the area, and restrictions on exhaust emissions dating from 1966, the problem remains (Table 2).

The distribution of smog in the Los Angeles area is extremely complex. Each primary chemical element involved in this brew—nitric oxide, carbon monoxide, sulfur dioxide, hydrocarbons—has a different distribution. Their concentrations are originally related to varying sources of pollution, but their distribution soon is effected by the prevailing winds—generally from the coast to inland areas, stronger in summer than winter, with their trajectories related to the topography. The volume of pollutants also varies both seasonally and hourly. Lower winter temperatures result in increased total fuel consumption. Substitution of fuel oil for limited quantities of natural gas in winter increases the quantities of nitric oxide and sulfur dioxide that are emitted in that season. Pollutants produced by automobiles reach their peak during the morning rush hour. Furthermore, the original contaminants react photochemically with the elements in the atmosphere to form secondary contaminants—nitrogen dioxide and ozone, for example—that have their own distribution patterns.

In the Los Angeles area the stationary sources of pollution—principally power generating plants, oil refineries, and heavy manufacturing—are located mainly in the south and southwest coastal area and in the east San Fernando Valley. These plants produce considerable quantities of sulfur dioxide and nitric oxide, the latter formed during the combustion of all fuels. While motor vehicle pollution is widespread, it is also heavily concentrated in the industrial areas mentioned above and, of course, in the central business district. Motor vehicles emit mainly carbon monoxide, nitric oxide, and hydrocarbons.

Carbon monoxide, a primary pollutant, comes almost entirely from automobiles. It has similar distributions in both summer and winter, although summer concentrations are generally lower as there are far fewer morning surface inversions during that season. During the winter morning traffic peak, for example, high concentrations of carbon monoxide are found over the Harbor Freeway, east of that area, and over the eastern portion of the San

Table 2. Contaminants, in Tons Per Day, from Major Sources Within Los Angeles County (Average Daily Emissions, 1971)

Sources	Hydrocarbons		Nitrogen Oxides	Particu-lates	Sulfur Dioxide	Carbon Monoxide
	Total	Reactive				
Industrial	640	130	130	40	175	10
Power Plants	5	—	100	5	35	—
Commercial	55	10	25	10	—	—
Residential	65	15	25	5	—	—
Motor Vehicles	1,620	1,170	755	55	35	8,960
Aircraft	80	30	15	15	5	135
Total (Rounded)	2,465	1,355	1,050	130	250	9,105

Source: Air Pollution Control District, Los Angeles County, *Profile of Air Pollution in Los Angeles County* (Los Angeles, 1971), p. 4.

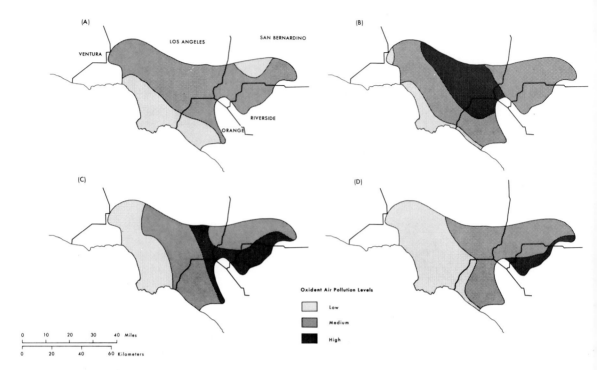

Figure 11. Distribution of oxidants. Based in part on Joseph V. Behar, "Simulation Model of Air Pollution Photo Chemistry," *Project Clean Air*, University of California Research Reports, vol. 4, Project 5-14, 1970, pp. 17-29.

Gabriel Valley. As the day progresses, levels do not increase, but the polluted air simply diffuses downwind.

Nitric oxide, a product of any fuel consumption, is highest in atmospheric concentration close to a major source area. Nitrogen dioxide, an intermediate product of photochemical reaction, is characterized by great seasonality. It reaches its greatest concentration in winter because with short days and less intense sunlight the reaction often fails to proceed beyond this stage. In summer, however, with intense sunlight present over many hours, the reaction usually continues to completion. During this season, when the prevailing winds sweep from the coast to the inland valleys, the coastal stations show relatively low nitrogen dioxide readings; the central area and east San Gabriel Valley, higher readings; and the more distant valleys, almost none.

The end product of the reaction discussed above—oxidants—has a pattern that is the most complicated of all, with maximum concentrations sometimes far from the source regions. Oxidant formation begins shortly after sunrise, but does not become a significant pollutant until all of the nitrogen dioxide from the morning traffic peak is consumed. Peak oxidant levels occur between noon and 2:00 P.M., with declining levels in the afternoon, and reach a minimum at night when oxidant formation stops due to lack of sunlight. The changing distribution of oxidant levels for four periods during the day—midmorning, late morning, early afternoon, and midafternoon—are shown in Figure 11. The varying pattern clearly reflects the effect of additional hours of sunlight as well as the gradual movement toward the eastern valleys in response to the prevailing daytime winds.

City Versus Suburbs

IMAGES

It is a popular pastime to suggest that Los Angeles is nothing more than "six suburbs in search of a city," and although the originator is lost in time, the saying lingers on. Does it have meaning today? It may be easier to understand the comment in a temporal context. If the comment originated, as some suggest, with Pirandello's play (*Six Characters in Search of an Author*) in the twenties when the population of the city was about 550,000 it may have been relevant, for at that time the Los Angeles area was a conglomeration of independent cities and widely spaced communities. The central city's boundaries were far flung; its "downtown" was modest in size and visually undistinguished.

Numerous independent cities developed at an early date with their own qualities and attractions. In the 1920s Long Beach was a thriving port and beach community, Pasadena was well known as a resort and retirement city attractively sited at the foot of the San Gabriels, and Santa Monica was already a growing beach municipality on Santa Monica Bay. Growth proceeded outward from all of these independent and semiindependent cities scattered irregularly in the region. In addition these cities were interconnected by one of the most extensive streetcar and interurban systems in the nation, and much traveling was done between them. Figure 12 indicates the far-flung nature of the connecting rail network. David Niven records that on his first visit to

southern California he seemed to travel for miles from Long Beach, where he landed, to Hollywood, and that he passed beanfields and oilfields along the way. This multifocussed urban region with large areas of intervening agricultural land would give an impression of suburban importance, particularly to the visitor (Figure 13).

Reinforcing this image was the extensive nature of the city of Los Angeles itself. Within the city limits were the centers of Wilmington and San Pedro, twenty miles to the south. These cities, like Hollywood to the north, had disincorporated and had been annexed to Los Angeles. The embryonic communities of Van Nuys and Lankershim (now known as North Hollywood) were north of the Santa Monica Mountains in the San Fernando Valley. And along Santa Monica Bay the communities of Venice and the Pacific Palisades fell within the city's corporate boundaries (Figure 14). Thus Los Angeles, at an early date, spread far and wide, absorbing many formerly independent communities and surrounding others —Beverly Hills and San Fernando—that maintained their political independence. These distant and loosely interconnected communities reinforced the feeling of an uncohesive metropolitan structure.

Further, the central business district of Los Angeles was without tall buildings and unimpressive in appearance. Until 1957 the city imposed a building height restriction of 150 feet on structures within its jurisdiction and no skyscrapers symbolized the commercial domi-

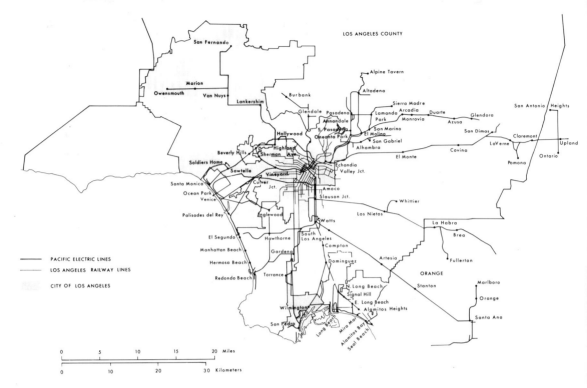

Figure 12. Interurban streetcar lines and urban development about 1925. Modified from: Robert M. Fogelson, *The Fragmented Metropolis—Los Angeles 1850–1930* (Cambridge, Mass.: Harvard University Press, 1967).

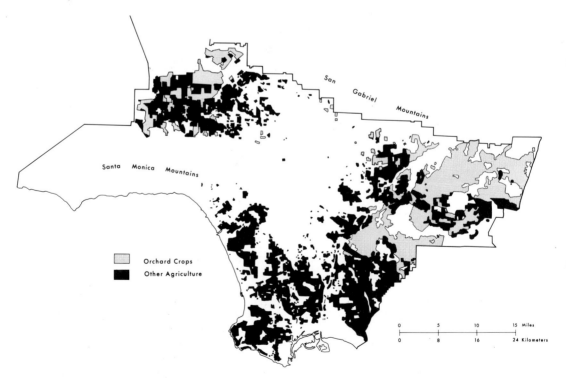

Figure 13. The distribution of agricultural land in 1939. County of Los Angeles Regional Planning Commission. Source: Land Use Survey (Los Angeles, 1940).

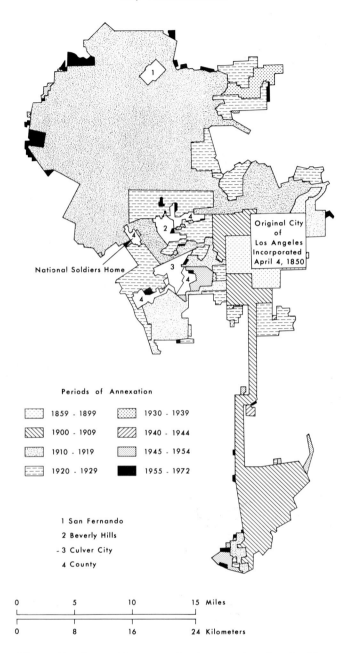

Figure 14. Date of incorporation by area, Los Angeles City.

nance of the center. Only the city hall was exempt, and it rose above the modestly sized commercial and financial structures. Actually, the central business district of the twenties belied its appearance in its function, for in 1920 the area was the home of 75 percent of Los Angeles' commercial and professional enterprise. And in 1924 a traffic survey showed

1.2 million persons a day, more than the entire population of the city, traveled to and from the central business district.

However, at this time the automobile was arriving in massive numbers, and rapid decentralization of the CBD was about to begin. Between 1923 and 1931 the population within a ten mile radius of the CBD expanded 50 percent, but the number of people entering the central business district increased only 15 percent. Symptomatic of the response of merchants to changing conditions, the largest department store in the city opened a branch, magnificent in style and furnishings, on Wilshire Boulevard, three and a half miles from its parent store. And as further evidence of increasing dispersal, UCLA, originally located in the central business district, moved in 1929 to a new campus in Westwood, a dozen miles from its original site.

Finally, the impression of a collection of suburbs in search of a city must have been closely related to the southern Californian's penchant for living in single family dwellings, the housing symbol of suburbia. As recently as 1950 almost 66 percent of the dwelling units were detached structures (Table 3). This compares with about 28 percent in the Chicago area, 20 percent in the New York area, and 15 percent in the Philadelphia area at the same date. To a visitor expecting the solid rows of apartments characteristic of cities of Europe or the East, Los Angeles indeed must have resembled a vast suburbia.

REALITY

But what image should a modern Pirandello evoke to convey the present reality of the Los Angeles landscape? Although the urbanized area today covers much more territory, the area familiar to the visitor of the twenties is now solidly built up with urban structures. The central city's "downtown" is evolving into a recog-

nizable urban center, and apartments have outnumbered single family units in the city's construction statistics since the 1950s. In short, in varying ways the urban area has evolved into a reasonably "average" metropolis, although items of individuality remain.

Over the past twenty years most urban areas have been characterized by a trend of decreasing urban population densities. This has largely come about through the growth of suburban areas outside of the old central cities and at least partly in response to generally rising household incomes and the availability of the automobile. Although gross residential density is only a rough measure of density, the averages for the United States do indicate that both for central cities and for suburban areas the urban densities have dropped over the past twenty years. But these averages mask some of the more interesting trends which emerge when we examine four large metropolitan areas. While the New York central city area has had stable or slightly increasing residential densities and declining suburban densities, Chicago has experienced significantly decreasing central densities and slightly increasing suburban densities, and Los Angeles has had increases in both central city and suburban densities (Table 4). We cannot extrapolate these figures too much, but it is reasonable to hypothesize that while other metropolitan areas approach Los Angeles in their density patterns, at the same time Los Angeles is becoming more like other metropolitan areas. We might conclude that the trends will bring to an end the still commonplace notion that service and community fa-

Table 3. Ratios of Single Family to Multiple Family Units in Los Angeles City and County, 1950–1970

	Single Family Units	(percent)	Mobile Homes	(percent)	Multiple Family Units	(percent)	Total Units
1970							
City	560,378	(52.0)	6,553	(0.6)	510,261	(47.4)	1,077,192
SMSA	1,545,178	(60.9)	35,685	(1.4)	957,274	(37.7)	2,538,137
1960							
City	533,103	(60.8)	4,365	(0.5)	339,265	(38.7)	876,733
SMSA	1,588,342	(71.7)	33,531	(1.5)	593,677	(26.8)	2,215,550
1950							
City	361,655	(54.8)	- - - - - -	- - - -	297,735	(45.2)	659,390
SMSA	925,880	(65.9)	- - - - - -	- - - -	478,670	(34.1)	1,404,550

Source: Censuses of Housing, 1950, 1960, 1970.

Table 4. Selected Residential Densities for the New York, Chicago, Los Angeles, and San Francisco Metropolitan Areas, 1950-1970

	1950	*1960*	*1970*
New York–Northeastern New Jersey			
Total urbanized area	*9,810*	*7,512*	*6,683*
Inside central cities	24,537	24,132	24,382
(New York City)	(25,046)	(25,966)	(26,343)
Outside central cities	4,066	3,541	3,580
Chicago–Northwestern Indiana			
Total urbanized area	*6,954*	*6,238*	*5,257*
Inside central cities	17,450	13,138	12,283
(Chicago)	(17,450)	(16,014)	(15,126)
Outside central cities	2,599	3,131	3,091
Los Angeles–Long Beach			
Total urbanized area	*4,587*	*4,633*	*5,313*
Inside central cities	4,370	5,475	6,135
(Los Angeles)	(4,370)	(5,447)	(7,364)
Outside central cities	4,821	4,134	4,818
San Francisco–Oakland			
Total urbanized area	*7,038*	*4,213*	*4,387*
Inside central cities	11,885	11,351	10,035
(San Francisco)	(17,385)	(16,307)	(15,764)
Outside central cities	4,545	2,734	3,252

Source: U.S. Censuses of Population, 1950, 1960, and 1970; and Donald Foley, *Accessibility for Residents in the Metropolitan Environment*, Institute of Urban and Regional Development, Working Paper no. 200, (Berkeley: University of California, 1965).

cilities will be within walking distance of most homes. Except for some children's activities, suburban densities in all major metropolitan areas are now so low as to preclude movements other than by automobile.

The once loosely knit communities have developed into a metropolis with urban densities comparable to many other American cities, as can be seen in Table 4. Further, suburban areas of Los Angeles exceed suburban densities in Chicago and New York. Within Los Angeles itself a broad area west of downtown, running all the way from Hollywood to the Santa Monica Freeway, has a density of over 15,000 persons per square mile, comparable to those found in the cities of Chicago or San Francisco. Smaller areas as diverse as Boyle Heights, the Sunset Strip, Westwood, and a portion of Long Beach have similar densities. Most of the rest of the nonindustrialized portions of the coastal plain, extending inland as far as Burbank and Glendale, have densities of from 10,000 to 15,000 persons per square mile. Densities in the San Fernando and San Gabriel valleys range from 5,000 to 10,000—respectably high figures for suburban areas. Only in the hilly areas (and in tracts occupied by industry) do densities fall below the 5,000 figure (Figure 15).

Continued areas of low density in Los Angeles are the result of several factors, but possibly most important of these is the persistence within the city of substantial areas which are underdeveloped and perhaps undevelopable. The Santa Monica Mountains, although infiltrated with fingers of residential usage, are essentially undeveloped. Further, even in 1973 there are other large tracts within the city being developed or redeveloped with significant effects on density. Many of these tracts—such as the oil fields of Baldwin Hills, the developments of Century City, or the open land near the Hughes airport—are in private hands.

An important element in the increasing density is the gradual shift from the dominance of the single family residence to multifamily structures. The city of Los Angeles now has about equal proportions of multiunit and single unit housing, while the county has only slightly

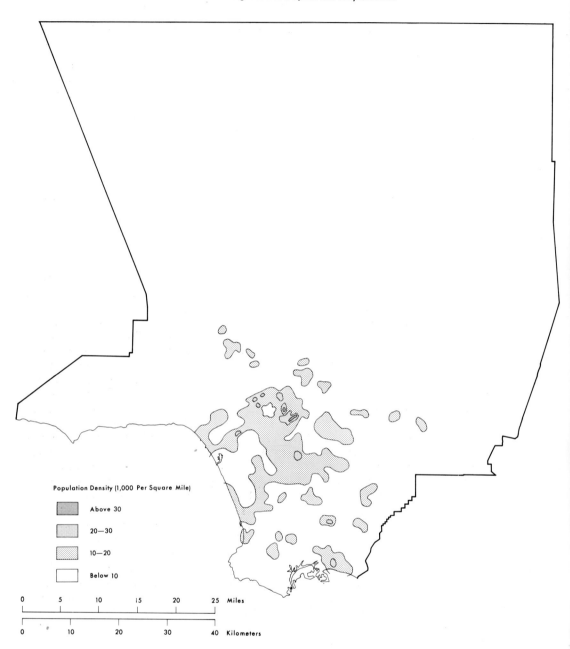

Figure 15. Population density. Data Source: Los Angeles County Regional Planning Commission.

more than twice as many single units as multiple units. This shift can be measured by noting the changing mix of rental versus owner units in the past decade. In the city of Los Angeles in 1960, 46 percent of the units were owner-occupied and 54 percent renter-occupied; in 1970 the proportions were 41 percent and 59 percent. Within the SMSA in 1960, 56 percent of the units were owner-occupied, 44 percent rented; by 1970 the figures were 54 and 46 percent (Table 5).

The central business district has also developed rapidly within the last decade and now has the appearance as well as the function of a metropolitan focus. Within the past decade a downtown building boom has resulted in the

Table 5. Renter and Owner Occupancy for Los Angeles City and County, 1950–1970

	Owner-Occupied Units	(Percent)	Renter-Occupied Units	(Percent)	Total Occupied Units
1970					
City	419,801	(40.9)	607,573	(59.1)	1,027,374
SMSA	1,179,943	(48.5)	1,252,038	(51.5)	2,431,981
1960					
City	404,962	(46.2)	471,806	(53.8)	876,768
SMSA	1,244,022	(56.1)	971,573	(43.9)	2,215,595
1950					
City	301,295	(45.7)	358,095	(54.3)	659,390
SMSA	755,880	(53.8)	648,670	(46.2)	1,404,550

Source: Censuses of Housing, 1950, 1960, 1970.

construction of a half dozen buildings ranging in height from forty-one to sixty-two stories. In addition, a new shopping mall was opened in 1973, including the largest department store to be built in any central city in forty years. A major civic-cultural center has been developing throughout the last decade, and there is also major residential redevelopment in the Bunker Hill section of the core.

A billion dollar building boom in downtown Los Angeles has not only created a new skyline, but has resulted in the relocation of a number of functions. The financial district now has more office space available (some still unoccupied) than San Francisco and has shifted from its traditional Spring Street location, on the east side of downtown, to new buildings on Flower and Figueroa streets. The locational change seems due to the attractiveness of sites adjacent to the Harbor Freeway, just south of the "interchange," the focus of the regional freeway system. Similarly, the retail section has become increasingly concentrated on Seventh Street, close to the freeway, while the older mass appeal stores on Broadway emphasize goods particularly appealing to the nearby inhabitants—Mexican Americans and blacks. Traditional "downtown" elements remain, with a garment center concentration on Los Angeles Street supported by a new California Apparel Mart. A produce market is located at Seventh and Central. Both of these latter elements are second in size only to those of New York. A Convention and Exhibition Center, completed in 1971, lies on the southern margin of the downtown area, but also adjacent to the Harbor Freeway.

The central core of Los Angeles is clearly the largest business center, with an estimated 240,000 employees in 1970 compared to 130,000 on Wilshire, 23,000 in Westwood, and 13,000 in Century City. But the renaissance of the downtown does not mean that Los Angeles is yet a city where activity is concentrated in a restricted area. Only 3 percent of the SMSA retail sales were in the Los Angeles CBD in 1963, as compared with 15.5 percent in Manhattan, 7.6 percent in Chicago, and 5.5 percent in Detroit. In the twelve year period 1960–1972, twenty-five office or residential structures were built in the downtown area and seventy-nine along the Whilshire corridor. And the "smart shops" and the specialty stores tend to locate on Wilshire Boulevard or in Beverly Hills. If one were to consider Wilshire Boulevard to be an extension of the central business district of the city (which would be comparable to using Manhattan as the CBD) it is likely that the Los Angeles picture would be similar to that of such cities as Chicago or Detroit.

THE ROLE OF COMMUNITIES IN THE METROPOLIS

Along with the commentary on the low density suburban nature and assumed sameness of the Los Angeles metropolitan area is the assumption that there is no significant community structure within the region. However, there are over 180 named communities recognized and included in city directories and maps. The most obvious are the independently incorporated cities such as Beverly Hills, Santa Monica, Long

Beach, and seventy-three other cities in Los Angeles County alone, that have legal sovereignty and governmental identity. But many of the unincorporated places also have long community traditions and traditional place names —Altadena, Calabasas, La Canada, and Malibu come readily to mind, along with the newer but just as distinctive Marina Del Rey.

Significantly, community identification seems as strong within the city of Los Angeles as in the suburban areas. Perhaps because of the way in which Los Angeles grew areally, often by annexing territory with some previous identity, community names remain officially attached to portions of the city. Hollywood was the earliest example of an area that retained its name as a post office address, although legally becoming a part of the city of Los Angeles. Many other communities followed the same procedure when they were annexed to the city. As far as both residents and postal authorities are concerned one lives not in Los Angeles, but in North Hollywood, Van Nuys, Encino, Woodland Hills, Canoga Park, Reseda, Chatsworth, Northridge, or Pacoima, to use some San Fernando Valley examples. In all, twenty community names appear in the state list of post offices as independent places, even though all are within Los Angeles.

Social commentators have suggested that with the fluidity of the population in the Los Angeles region, the ease with which people move through the neighborhoods, and the impact of the freeway, which gives people access to the whole city, there is less need to have strong ties with their immediate neighborhood. However, in a recent survey the sample population were able not only to identify their neighborhood, but they expressed satisfaction with it. Seventy-five percent of the whole population expressed satisfaction with the neighborhood in which they were then living. The percentage was lower for blacks—44 percent—and Mexican-Americans—58 percent. The lower percentage of the black population who were satisfied relates almost certainly to the lower quality of housing available in areas of black concentrations and the desire of many blacks to live in areas which have a mix of populations.

For example, in the same survey, 66 percent of the blacks responded that people should be different within communities. But even more impressive in terms of the importance of the community, almost 70 percent of the Mexican-Americans, 65 percent of the blacks, and 61 percent of the whites made the statement, "I feel a part of my neighborhood." (This question was asked after they had already given a name to their particular neighborhood.) The figures imply a relatively strong sense of neighborhood, stronger for Mexican-Americans than whites but relatively strong for all three groups. This is further expressed in the percentages of people who say that they would like to remain in their present neighborhood. These stayers ranged from 60 percent for blacks to 67 percent for Mexican-Americans.

A more specific study of the small community of Mar Vista, located in the western part of the Los Angeles metropolitan area, also reveals the importance of the local neighborhood to its residents. In a survey of this particular community 80 percent of the population had lived in Los Angeles for more than ten years and 55 percent of the population had lived in the Mar Vista community for more than ten years. Further, maps which show the percent of the population who did not live in the same house as five years ago do not suggest that Los Angeles is significantly different from other metropolitan areas.

PLACES AND COMMUNITIES: PERCEPTIONS AND QUALITY

The stereotype of the Los Angeles region as an area of "endless streets . . . endless houses, clustered in indistinguishable neighborhoods," has been discussed previously and countered with examples of specific physical variety. But this alleged lack of diversity, paucity of "placiness," and scarcity of neighborhood identity also fails when tested with some simple measures of residential areas in the region.

There are three major ways of viewing the residential population patterns of a city. One relates to the economics of housing and residential values. A second involves the perceptions of individuals, their feelings and responses to areas of the city. A third view involves the quality of the environment as reflected in a set of variables such as crime, substandard housing, and garbage collection.

A map of housing values is the simplest and, in many ways, the most instructive view of any city. In these objective terms Los Angeles seems similar to many other metropolitan areas (Figure 16). Near the center of the city are the low-

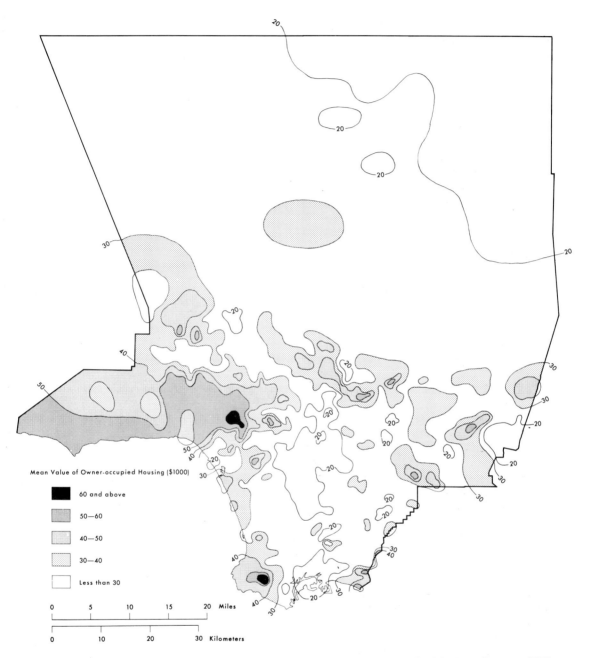

Figure 16. Mean value of owner-occupied housing in the Los Angeles SMSA. Data Source: 1970 Census of Housing.

est valued residences—although this area is not circular but rather an elongated rectangular sector. Successive increases in values of housing form irregular ring-shaped (although not strictly circular) additions around this low value core. The highest value residences (with a median value of $50,000) are located at the outer edges of the metropolitan area. However, this highest value area is not continuous and has its greatest concentration coincident with the Santa Monica Mountains, from the Hollywood Hills in the east to the Pacific Palisades and Malibu in the west. The most serious distortions of the general pattern described above are the distribution of areas of homes which range in value from $30,000 to $35,000. Locations of census tracts with values in this range are found interspersed throughout the city and county.

A quite different approach to the variety of places within the region is based on the way in which individuals rate communities. A simple procedural approach is to ask people to rank a number of communities, in order, in which they would most like to live. To make this test even more realistic a constraint was added—that the choice had to be related to family income. Thus, the persons questioned must make their choices within a set of communities in which they would in actuality be able to purchase a house or rent an apartment. Figure 17 is a summary of the first choices of 1,024 persons, the heavily shaded areas being chosen by the greatest number of people.

Communities which are highly preferred comprise a number of distinctive regions. First, there is a ridge extending from Santa Monica in the west to Hollywood in the east. These communities include Santa Monica, West Los Angeles, Westwood Village, Beverly Hills, and Hollywood. The choice of these communities can be related to the quality of life in this region. The area is physically attractive, with large amounts of open green space and good access to the ocean and mountains. Several well-developed employment centers exist within the region and, in addition, there is a wide variety of shopping and entertainment facilities. The region is relatively smog free, with fewer smoggy days than the rest of the Los Angeles basin. The overall attractiveness of the area is reflected in higher rents and house values (Figure 6). A similarly attractive area, chosen by forty-nine persons, includes the beach towns of Redondo Beach, Manhattan Beach, Hermosa

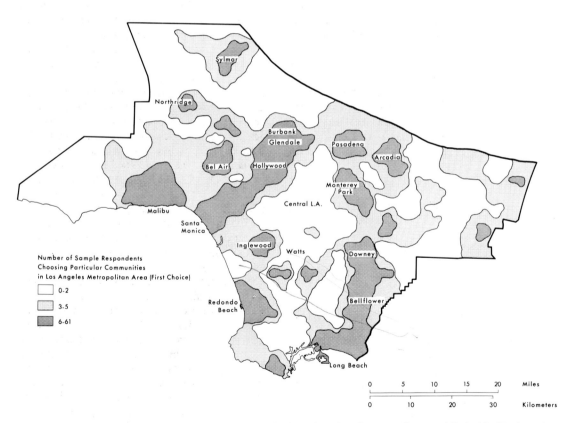

Figure 17. First preference communities within Los Angeles County. Source: W. A. V. Clark and Martin Cadwallader, "Residential Preferences: An Alternative View of Intraurban Space," *Environment and Planning* 5 (1973): pp. 693-703.

Beach, and the communtiy of Torrance. The attraction in this case is related to the lifestyle associated with beach communities or communities with good access to the beach.

A second highly preferred region made up of several communities in the eastern portion of the Los Angeles basin has a different set of explanations. The communities of Pasadena, Monterey Park, Alhambra, and Arcadia were all chosen by large numbers of persons. The choice of Pasadena probably relates to its preeminence as a residential area in times past, while that of Arcadia is related to newer housing opportunities. Alhambra is a middle income white community, but Monterey Park is a community preferred by Mexican-American households. Another highly preferred area includes the communities from Long Beach in the south to Bellflower and Downey in the northeast. The northward extension of this belt, which includes some poorer quality housing (in objective terms), is related to the residential preference of lower income whites, blacks, and Mexican-Americans. We can use the same logic to explain the choice of Inglewood near the Los Angeles Airport.

The least preferred areas are those near the center of the city and large portions of the San Fernando Valley. Despite the smog problem associated with much of the East Valley, the rapid expansion of new relatively low cost housing, especially in the last twenty years, would lead one to believe that the valley would be a more highly preferred area. It is a curious paradox.

A further analysis of choices showed that many persons preferred either the community they were living in or one nearby. Of the sixteen people who chose Pasadena, twelve were already living there; and of the fifteen people who chose Sherman Oaks, thirteen were already living there. Furthermore, many of those who did not choose their own community chose one nearby. Even communities like Santa Monica and Long Beach, which attracted preferences from widely scattered segments of the Los Angeles basin, were most often chosen by persons living nearby.

Residents of the Los Angeles area separate the supposedly amorphous city into distinct neighborhoods. Moreover, they indicate considerable identification with and knowledge of the locational aspects of their home neighborhoods. It is likely, however, that they lack complete information about more distant neighborhoods. Their judgments reflect an inability to know all the communities in a very large metropolitan area.

THE BEST AND WORST PLACES TO LIVE

A different approach to the understanding of the widely varying neighborhood structures was reported in a study by the Los Angeles Community Analysis Bureau. The objective of the study was to rank the communities within the city of Los Angeles in terms of the quality of urban life. Data were collected for a variety of variables and treated statistically to yield a measure of the blight of each of sixty-five communities which have been delimited for the city.

The variables were grouped into four general categories. The first was *community ambience,* which included measures of per capita income, household income, percent sound housing, percent white collar employment, and owner occupancy of single family homes; the second, *urban stress variables,* included measures of suicides, arrests, and childhood diseases; the third, *alienation variables,* included items such as structural fires, minority school enrollment, percent of households with over 1.51 persons per room, high school dropouts, and traffic arrests. The final group of variables, identified as *poverty variables,* included measures of welfare, families receiving aid to dependent children, and also measures of housing without plumbing, and of unemployment.

The lowest ranked communities lie near the center of the city and in the southern extension of Los Angeles—areas with high percentages of minorities (Figure 18). Watts is a largely black, low income community with older small houses, a landscape quite different from low income tenement housing areas of eastern and midwestern cities. Indeed, the small frame house with a small yard seems incongruous to many visitors who associate minority ghettos with high density squalor, dirt, and decay. Boyle Heights is a counterpart community for the Mexican-American population and is surrounded by freeways and industry. Again, most of the housing is single family, with median values of $17,000 and median rents of $72.00 per month. Exposition Park is an older resi-

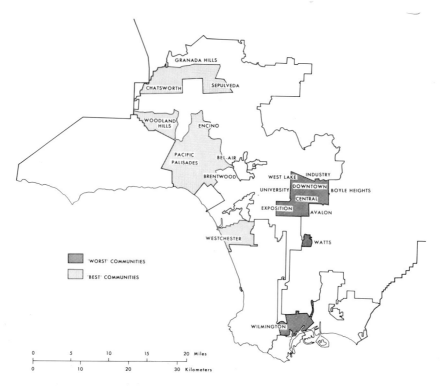

Figure 18. Location of "best" and "worst" communities within the city of Los Angeles. Adapted from Data Analysis Division, Community Analysis Bureau, City of Los Angeles, 1971.

dential section, a recent inmigration area for minorities, principally blacks.

At the other extreme are the outlying communities of Woodland Hills, Encino, Granada Hills, Pacific Palisades, Bel Air, and Brentwood. These are the communities with the highest per capita incomes, the most years of college, and the highest median home values and the highest median rents. In addition they are the areas which are considered among the most attractive physical areas within the city. Some are near the ocean, others are near or within the Santa Monica or Santa Susana mountains. The houses are large and frequently have swimming pools.

Midway between these extremes are the communities of West Los Angeles, West Wilshire, Sylmar, and Baldwin Hills. Not unexpectedly, these communities include a wide variety of locations both in the basin (that is, the pre-1950 development) and within the San Fernando Valley. West Los Angeles and West Wilshire are communities with a significant portion of older houses. Sylmar is quite different

from the other communities both in its location and residential patterns. Apart from the devastating impact of the 1971 earthquake, Sylmar is a quiet, lower middle income community with little industry and a population which commutes to the central San Fernando Valley or Los Angeles basin for employment opportunities. Baldwin Hills is a higher status area with more professional workers and homes with median values of $40,000. The area was largely built up in the 1940s and today has become an attractive community for minority professional populations seeking alternative lifestyles to those offered in Avalon, Watts, and the traditional locations available for minorities.

Two summary statements can be made about this multiple objective classification of communities. First, the classification closely follows the pattern of housing values already discussed. Second, the classification is a way of measuring some noneconomic phenomena and their impact on residential desirability.

The Changing Impact of Minorities

Metropolitan Los Angeles in the 1970s, as other large American urban centers, has a cosmopolitan population. The area is the home of some 1.7 million persons of Spanish heritage, mainly Mexican-Americans, 830,000 blacks, 120,000 Japanese-Americans, and 36,000 American Indians. The Mexican-American population is the largest urban concentration of Mexicans in the world outside of Mexico City. Only New York, Chicago, and Philadelphia have a larger number of blacks. The Japanese-American population is the largest concentration on the American mainland; and no urban area has more Indians. There are large Chinese (45,000), Philipino (40,000), and Korean colonies as well. In addition, nearly 600,000 Jews live in the area, third in the world to New York City and Tel Aviv. Further, about 29 percent of the inhabitants of the area are immigrants or second generation Americans. It would seem that the image of the area as a home of provincial midwesterners is mistaken, at least today.

A provincial image would have been erroneous a century ago as well, for during that period Los Angeles was fully as cosmopolitan as it is today. Ludwig Salvator, the Archduke of Austria, in his 1878 volume, *Eine Blume aus dem Goldenen Lande: oder, Los Angeles* (A flower from the golden land of Los Angeles), reported that the residents of the county were about equally divided among Americans, Europeans, and Californians (Mexicans), and "on the streets are heard spoken English, French, Spanish, German, and Italian." As Mc Williams points out, "Long before Iowans invaded Southern California . . . Polish intellectuals, British remittance men, Chinese immigrants, Basque sheep-herders, French and German peasants, and German-Jewish merchants and financiers were on the scene."

However, southern California essentially missed the inpouring of the vast throngs of European immigrants that engulfed eastern and midwestern cities in the late nineteenth and early twentieth centuries. As a result, Los Angeles did not experience an era of large ethnic enclaves so typical of many other American cities. While many cities came to be dominated by immigrant European Catholics, Los Angeles was filling up with mainly Protestant settlers from the states "back East." And the original open and polyglot atmosphere was replaced with a narrow, provincial aura. "Virtue has become virulent," lamented a resident in 1913.

A second distinguishing feature of the Los Angeles area through the years was the continued presence of a Mexican-American minority, a minority that has grown rapidly in the twentieth century. This Spansih-speaking population was for years relatively powerless, isolated, and, save for a few individuals, almost invisible. Mexican-Americans have not influenced Los Angeles in the same way the Irish affected Boston, or the Italians San Francisco, or the Jews New York.

THE RETURN OF THE MEXICAN

The Los Angeles area was a part of Mexico for its first seventy years; the names on the land

and of many of its streets and cities are Spanish; and Mexican-Americans have been its largest minority throughout its 200 year history. Yet the original Spanish-speaking inhabitants of the area had been almost absorbed by the invading Anglo until large scale migration from Mexico began early in the twentieth century. Revolutions in Mexico beginning in 1919 strengthened the flow, as did continuing efforts by Americans seeking laborers for railroad construction and maintenance; migratory agricultural labor; and workers for the expanding citrus industry, the brick, tile, and cement plants, and as general laborers everywhere. There were about 90,000 persons either born in Mexico or with parents born in Mexico in the area in 1920, and by 1930 the figure had tripled to 275,000. Today, the region's 1.7 million persons of Spanish heritage (perhaps 80 percent Mexican-American) comprise a proportion comparable to that of the black population in large eastern metropolitan areas.

The Mexican-Americans represent both the oldest and newest groups in Los Angeles, a situation made for irony. In the decades prior to World War II, migrant farm workers would converge on Los Angeles each winter. The local newspapers would regularly proclaim the event a "Mexican problem" and deplore the relief and hospital load created by this annual influx. Mexican-Americans long were barred from municipal pools, and as late as 1943 the area was the scene of "zoot suit" race riots, directed especially toward Mexican-American boys who wore this distinctive style of clothing. But during the same period the area was actively discovering and romanticizing its Spanish heritage. Starting with Helen Hunt Jackson's *Ramona,* a myth was created glorifying an imaginary life of the "mission days" (an activity which, incidentally, resurrected their crumbling remains). By 1900 this movement was well under way, symbolized in that year by the construction of a hotel in Riverside that became famous as the "Mission Inn." Its style of architecture was copied widely by builders throughout southern California. Further, numerous cities sponsored annual fiesta days, often including a colorful pageant called the ride of the *Rancheros Visitadores.* This is seen today in a different form in the bands of riders with embroidered suits and tasseled sombreros, seated on silver-encrusted saddles, who embellish the Tournament of Roses Parade in Pasadena each New Year's Day.

The current pattern of distribution of the Mexican-American population also has its anomalies. Early studies show that the Mexican-Americans (along with the Orientals) were more severely segregated than blacks. Today, however, their "ghettoization" is not as complete. A recent survey indicated that only about 10 percent of the Mexican-American population lived in census tracts where the population was more than 75 percent Mexican. Fully one-third of the Mexican population lived in tracts where the population was 15 percent or less Mexican-American, and another third lived in census tracts which were 45 percent Mexican-American. But as Figure 19 illustrates, distinct *barrios* do exist. The central *barrio*—where Mexican-Americans have replaced a Jewish population in Boyle Heights, City Terrace, and the adjacent communities of Lincoln Heights and East Los Angeles—is the nation's largest, and here Mexican-Americans account for about three-fourths of the population. Along Brooklyn Avenue and Whittier Boulevard enterprises are located that supply Mexican food, movies, professional services, immigration consulting, and so on. Rapid urbanization, too, has engulfed other previously outlying Mexican settlements—the "Latin towns" of railroad workers, clusters of agricultural laborers (as at Pacoima in the San Fernando Valley), and a colony (formerly walled!) of brickyard workers, now part of Montebello. Too, most of the towns in the citrus belts had their cluster of Mexicans, often literally "across the tracks."

The recent Mexican immigrant in Los Angeles is providing the area with its closest approximation of the earlier European settler of the eastern cities. Yet there appear to be some significant differences. The Mexican often has arrived after a rather inexpensive land journey, meaning to return to his homeland if dissatisfied. He is not always a legal immigrant and, even if he is, he is slow in becoming naturalized or simply disinterested in the process. He is in no hurry to give up the Spanish language. He does not seek quickly to abandon his cultural values. He has proven difficult to "melt" in the American "melting pot," and, after all, has arrived at a time when the value of blending is being questioned by many.

The Mexican-American in Los Angeles has been described by some as being almost invisible, part of a dual lifestyle, in an unseeing city. Yet in an "Anglo" city, the presence of the Mexican-American is ubiquitous. Now more

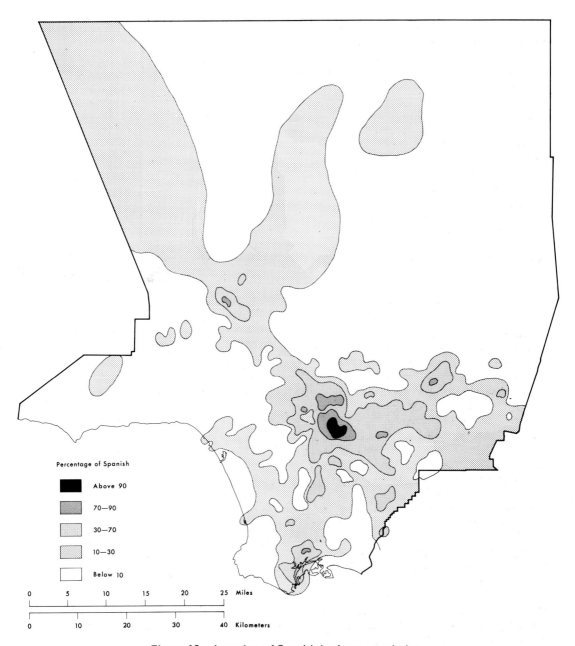

Figure 19. Location of Spanish-heritage population.

than 85 percent urban, he himself is "seen" whenever laborers are present, from construction project to assembly line. Mexican restaurants are widespread; Mexican food is present in every supermarket; and tacos, burritos and enchiladas are standard items in every school cafeteria, factory vending machine, or institutional food stand. Twist the dial of a television set or radio and Spanish voices are heard on several stations. A dozen or more theaters show Mexican films, the daily Spanish-language newspaper *La Opinion* circulates widely, and Dodger baseball games are broadcast in Spanish as well as in English. In addition, Spanish is increasingly taught as the second language in schools. And it probably was not entirely coincidental that one of the rare disturbances of the 1960s on a local university campus occurred on *Cinco de Mayo* May 5), the anniversary of Mexico's victory over a foreign tyrant and a day of celebration throughout the Mexican-American community.

BLACKS DISCOVER SOUTHERN CALIFORNIA

Although the Los Angeles neighborhood of Watts blazed to worldwide fame as a black ghetto in 1968, and although Central Avenue was a nationally known black street in the 1920s, the black component of the population is generally of modest proportions and recent in arrival. Though blacks were an important element in the original settlement of Los Angeles (1781), they had dwindled to a mere dozen in a city of 1,600 persons in 1850. The modern black community had its beginnings in the expansive period of the 1880s during which blacks increased from 102 to 1,285 and to some 2.5 percent of the population. Significantly, this proportion changed only slightly during the next half century. That the 2,841 blacks in Los Angeles in 1900 made it the largest black settlement on the Pacific Coast is an indication of the small attraction the region had for blacks in the early years.

Black neighborhoods in Los Angeles were widely dispersed in the decades around the turn of the century, housing a population that reached 7,500 in the rapidly growing city of 1910. One black neighborhood developed on the southeastern edge of the business district (along Weller Street between First and Second), and others formed in several directions from downtown—along Temple Avenue to the northwest, in Boyle Heights on the northeast, along Jefferson Boulevard on the west (between Normandie and Western), and in a far-flung outlier to the south called the "Furlong Tract" (between 51st and 55th, and Alameda and Central avenues). Perhaps this generally widespread pattern of residences was the result of the small population of the city, its rapid expansion, and the relatively small amount of old housing located in any one area. These same factors, however, did not prevent a much higher degree of segregation among the few Japanese and Chinese (and the more numerous Mexican-Americans) in the city.

But by 1920, although the proportion of blacks to whites was no larger than it had been forty years previously, most blacks were living in a spatial ghetto. It now stretched about thirty blocks down Central Avenue from the original downtown settlement. The city of Watts at this time was a new small rural outlier. (Watts, incidentally, was annexed by Los Angeles in 1926.) This marked change in residential pattern was due to the increased use of deed restrictions and other forms of white resistance. However, the ghetto itself in this decade was still quite mixed in its population with many whites interspersed among the blacks. Central Avenue with its churches and businesses became one of the most notable "Negro streets" in the country. By 1925 the main black community had reached Slauson Avenue, which was to remain an impenetrable barrier until World War II. For fifteen years this area of black residences was surrounded by established white areas closed to black occupancy by restrictive covenants, although the black population of the city expanded to about 65,000 by 1940. Efforts to establish black residences in some of the beach cities were also effectively blocked.

The booming growth during World War II and its aftermath also saw the beginning of a change in black-white ratios of fifty years duration. In Los Angeles County the white population increased by 41 percent in the decade of the 1940s, the black population increased by 112 percent, and blacks accounted for 5.5 percent of the total by 1950. Similarly, in the decades of the 1950s and the 1960s the proportion of blacks increased significantly—to 7.6 percent in 1960 and 10.8 percent in 1970. However, these ratios are far lower than those of the metropolitan areas of Chicago and Detroit, 19 percent; or New York and Philadelphia, 18 percent. Similarly, the central city, Los Angeles, due mainly to its vast areal extent, has a population which is only about 18 percent black, far lower than most cities in its size class.

Spatially, the decade of the forties saw a breaching of the Slauson Avenue barrier, although the density of the black population remained vastly higher north of that street than immediately south of it, and it also witnessed a large increase of the black population in the Watts area. A Jefferson Avenue outlier also expanded, and some significant black population also appeared in the suburbs, particularly in an area of older black settlement in western Pasadena–Altadena.

By 1960 the three largest black neighborhoods–Central Avenue-Furlong Tract, Watts, and West Jefferson–had coalesced. Today it stands as a massive segregated area, stretching from the southern part of downtown Los Angeles southward more than a dozen miles, and reaching from three to seven miles westward (Figure 20). Alameda Street, with its

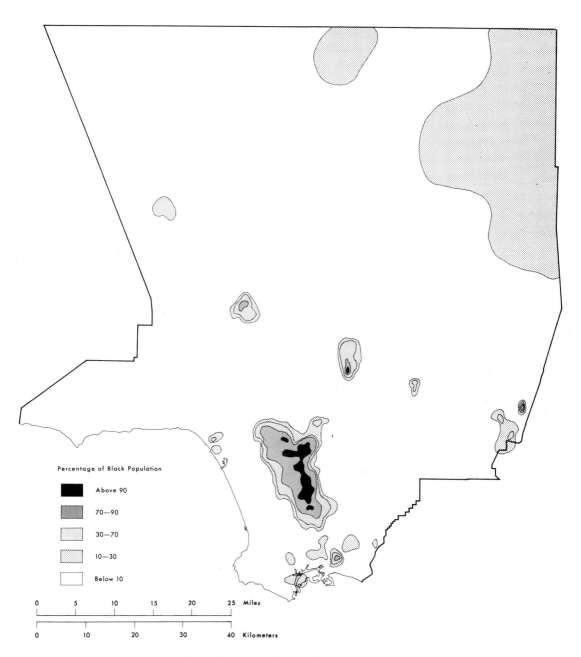

Figure 20. Location of black population.

railroad tracks (and generally unfriendly white suburban cities beyond), has been a stable eastern boundary through the years and expansion has been southward and westward. Much of the area is within the city of Los Angeles or unincorporated county territory (the Willowbrook district, for example), but near the southern limit the city of Compton is 71 percent black (and in this city blacks do live east of Alameda), and on the west the borders of Inglewood (11 percent black) have been reached. To the northeast the ghetto is "merging into and possibly transforming" an area predominantly Jewish in population. The Pasadena-Altadena "ghettolette" (beginning with a settlement of domestics and gardeners handy to that community in the 1880s) has also grown and 16 percent of the Pasadena population is black, as is 27 percent of the unincorporated adjacent community of Altadena.

As is to be expected in an area of nearly forty square miles, much variety is present in the main ghetto of south central Los Angeles, and even its older and meaner areas do not have the appearance of slums in the usual sense. The Harbor Freeway bisects the area and, generally speaking, the older and poorer areas are to the east, particularly the original Furlong Tract and the Watts neighborhood. Even here, however, there are no tenements, two-thirds of the dwellings are single family houses (occasionally run-down, rented shacks), and even the public housing development consists of one or two story stucco buildings. West of the freeway much of the area is distinctly middle class, and on its northwestern edge in the Baldwin Hills area takes in some fine homes, often with swimming pools.

Yet the standards of living and economic opportunities are still limited. According to the 1970 census the median income for black families was $7,500; for Spanish-surname families, $8,900; and for white families, $11,400. As in other metropolitan areas, whites are significantly better off than blacks, and in the Los Angeles case the Spanish-surname population is in an intermediate position. Not unrelated is the segregation of education in Los Angeles. Approximately 96 percent of black students in Los Angeles attend predominantly black elementary and high schools. Dropout rates in high schools are approximately 27–54 percent for black high schools and 1–34 percent for white high schools. The conclusions suggest that the minorities, although somewhat better off because of the ameliorating effects of climate and the higher percent of single family and homeowner occupied units, are still disadvantaged with respect to the white majority.

JAPANESE—OUT OF THE FIELDS AND INTO THE OFFICE

Japanese migrants to America early showed a preference for the Los Angeles area and from 1910 to the present it has had the largest Japanese agglomeration on the mainland. Early arrivals were fishermen and farmers, with settlements in habor and rural areas, although the center of life was a "Little Tokyo" section in downtown Los Angeles. After Pearl Harbor the Japanese—citizen and alien alike—were forcibly resettled away from the coast but most returned after the war even though they were not compensated for their huge financial losses.

Today there are perhaps 120,000 Americans of Japanese descent in the Los Angeles area. Little Tokyo still exists, graced with several high-rise office structures financed with Japanese capital and the location of the Hongwanji Buddhist Temple, the head temple of the fifteen Buddhist churches in southern California. But it is now mainly an ethnic and tourist shopping center—the location of Japanese restaurants, groceries, shops, and other businesses. Japanese residential life is partially concentrated in several other areas, including the area adjacent to Crenshaw Square (at Crenshaw and Jefferson), a Nisei (second generation Japanese-American) developed shopping center near the Town and Country shopping center in Gardena, and around Sawtelle Boulevard in West Los Angeles, the location of several Japanese churches (Figure 21). But in general the Japanese have been freed from ghetto restrictions and live throughout the Los Angeles metropolis.

One writer has asserted that the Japanese in Los Angeles make up a miniature New York Jewish community. Cultural values emphasizing hard work and achievement have been coupled with effective use of the public school system, including higher education opportunities in law, finance, and medicine. The Japanese nursery and gardener still exist but are no longer necessarily typical, although the Japanese style of garden with its clean simple style

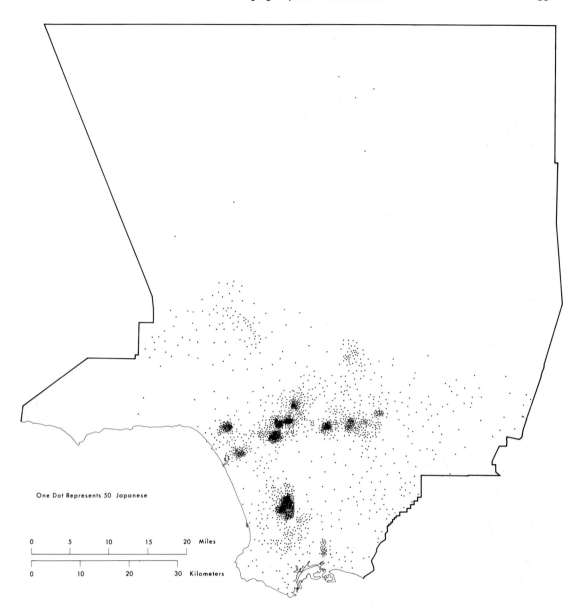

Figure 21. Location of Japanese population.

and serene feeling has a marked influence on landscaping throughout the area.

DIASPORA IN THE SUN

Los Angeles today has considerable Diaspora status as the home of nearly one of every ten American Jews. The *Jewish American Yearbook* estimates that the 1972 Jewish population of Los Angeles County was 535,000 and of Orange County, 30,000, with lesser numbers in other suburban areas. Although this represents only a small proportion of the total population (6 percent, only half that of New York), the Jewish population has been influential in the motion picture industry, the apparel industry is largely a Jewish business, and Jewish businessmen are important in the consumer goods, wholesale trade, and the building industries. Much of the Jewish influx has occurred in re-

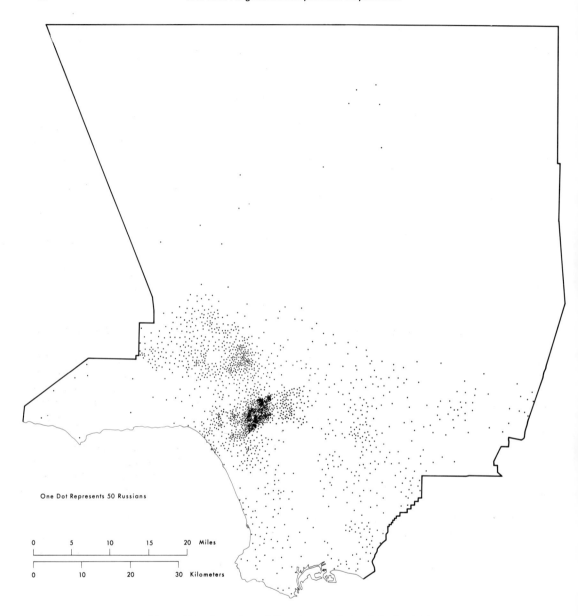

One Dot Represents 50 Russians

Figure 22. Location of Russian stock (mainly Jewish).

cent decades and has added a traditionally urbanizing force to the area's population.

A Jewish element was important in the early days of Los Angeles, with Horace Bell reporting in the early 1850s that "most of the merchants were Jews." But total numbers were few—an estimated 2,500 in 1900 and a modest 20,000 twenty years later. However, with an increasing Jewish population, dis-

tinctive neighborhoods developed. Temple Street reportedly was the Jewish main street in 1910, followed by a section of Central Avenue during the next decade. But even by 1920 more prosperous and acculturated Jews were moving westward into such areas as Wilshire, West Adams, and Hollywood.

During the twenties the Jewish population more than tripled (to 70,000) and then doubled again in the thirties (150,000). The main area of influx during the boom years of the twenties, accommodating immigrants mainly from Russia, Poland, and Germany, was east of downtown, across the Los Angeles River and the railroad tracks, in Boyle Heights and adjacent areas. Here, along Brooklyn and Wabash avenues, and in the nearby City Terrace district, bona fide Jewish neighborhoods developed. Yiddish was the language of the streets, and Saturdays and Jewish holidays were noted for closed businesses and a festive appearance. While Boyle Heights was still an important Jewish community in the 1930s, additional neighborhoods on the west side—Central Wilshire and West Pico—became significant areas of residence. Fairfax Avenue, north of Wilshire, in the center of an apartment district, became the Jewish shopping street and still is today, although many of its current patrons belong to an older generation.

Jewish migration was an important part of the World War II and postwar surge of people to the Los Angeles area. By 1940 it was estimated that the Jewish population had reached the quarter million mark and for a brief period arriving Jews were thought to account for at least one-eighth of the total inmigration. Boyle Heights and other east side neighborhoods have now been abandoned to other residents, particularly Mexican-Americans. Generally many of the older west side and newer adjoining west side nieghborhoods have coalesced. An area extending from Hollywood to Wilshire, and from Beverly Hills to Cheviot Hills, perhaps five square miles in all and consisting of some twenty-one census tracts, has an estimated Jewish population ranging from 30 to 100 percent. Further dispersion has occurred, to the high class neighborhoods of Westwood, Brentwood, and the Pacific Palisades. The suburban San Fernando Valley is the home of more than 125,000 Jews, particularly the communities along its southern margin—Studio City, Sherman Oaks, Encino, Tarzana, and Woodland Hills (Figure 22).

In Los Angeles, as in other metropolitan centers, there is evidence of an increasing concentration of minorities in the central city. Already 18 percent black and almost 19 percent of Spanish heritage, projections have the Spanish-heritage population outnumbering the "census white" category by 1990, with two-thirds of the population being composed of ethnic minorities. Further, it is suggested that blacks and Spanish-heritage population will comprise a majority of the Los Angeles County population as early as 1980. Thus both Los Angeles City and the county seem to be developing a similar racial structure to other metropolitan areas, with an ethnic core and surrounding white suburbs.

The possibility of Los Angeles County becoming an area of ethnic majority is due largely to the high percentage of Spanish-heritage population. However, the trend is also affected by the scattered but growing concentrations of black families in the outlying nodes of Pasadena, Santa Monica, Long Beach, Pacoima, and Fontana. While other metropolitan areas have faced the increasing concentrations of minority families for some years, if not decades, the rise of a minority population is much more recent in Los Angeles. There may still be opportunities to reverse the central-suburban dichotomy and to increase the possibilities for black families to live in suburban nodes other than those now occupied.

The Spatial Structure of Economic Activities*

Employment location patterns of various economic activities in Los Angeles County provide further evidence that the area is hardly unique, but in broad outline similar to other large American metropolitan areas. There are differences; the activities are much more spread out, reflecting the fact that development occurred during the era of the automobile. But as the maps in Figures 23, 24, and 25 show, it is almost as if a New York or a Chicago had been placed on a stretching frame. The relative locations of activities remain unchanged, but in Los Angeles the distances between places have been increased. The simple geographical principles of concentration and dispersion still apply.

In order to comprehend the major patterns of economic activity, specifically the location of jobs, within the Los Angeles basin, the region is subdivided into labor market areas which roughly correspond to recognized communities within Los Angeles County. Economic activities are divided into seven categories—financial, government, transportation and communication, wholesaling, retailing, service, and manufacturing. The relative importance of each activity as a resource of employment is measured in terms of the number of jobs created by firms in each category. Because some of the patterns are very similar, the seven activities can be summarized by three composite maps (Figures 23, 24, and 25).

CONCENTRATED ACTIVITIES

There is a downtown focus in Los Angeles and hundreds of thousands of people work there, even if many of them shop elsewhere. The outward expansion of Los Angeles has not been matched by firms in certain categories, notably finance and wholesaling (Figure 23). The continued concentration of jobs in both categories in or near the central Los Angeles area suggests that the city center for all its drawbacks—such as crime and congestion, not to mention the high land values—is still a very desirable place to locate for certain activities.

Finance, with 43 percent of its employees working in the central Los Angeles area, has never spread far from its initial focus. Neither old nor new firms can afford to choose a location very far from the financial district because the industry as a whole is highly interconnected and dependent upon almost instantaneous exchange, both of money and information, which can often only be achieved through face-to-face contact. Under such conditions, physical proximity to such centralized facilities as the stock exchange and other firms in the industry is almost a necessity.

The only significant clustering of firms locating outside the financial district is along Wilshire Boulevard. There is a certain status value attached to a Wilshire Boulevard location which is particularly attractive to firms, such as insurance companies, whose stock in trade is public image. There are, however, financial activities which are consumer oriented. Thus the patterns of banks and savings and loan com-

*This section was contributed by Professor James Huff of the Department of Geography, UCLA.

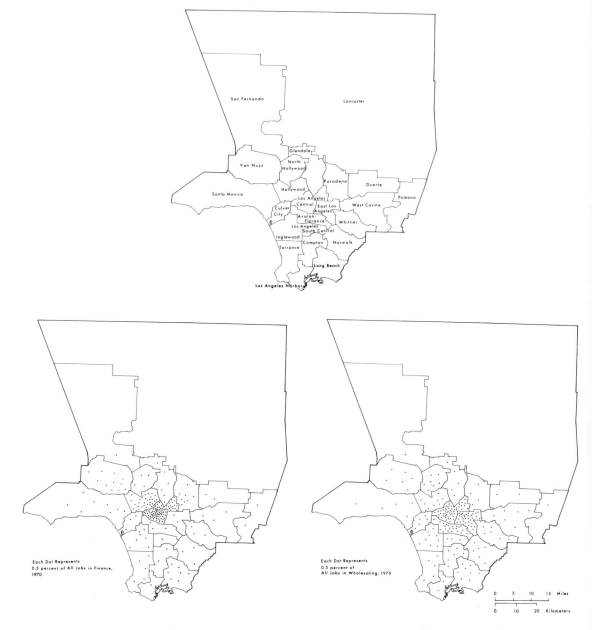

Figure 23. The distribution of finance and wholesaling employment, 1970.

panies are similar to the distribution of population within the metropolitan area if one allows for distortions caused by discrepancies in the median incomes of the various communities.

Finance is not the only activity which is highly concentrated in the downtown area. The distribution of goods is also attracted to the center of the city, but for very different reasons. One need only look at a map of the metropolitan area's highway network (Figure 26) to understand why the wholesale trade, trucking, and warehousing industries are located in the central portion of the city. Although growth of the transport system has probably been the most important factor contributing to the outward expansion

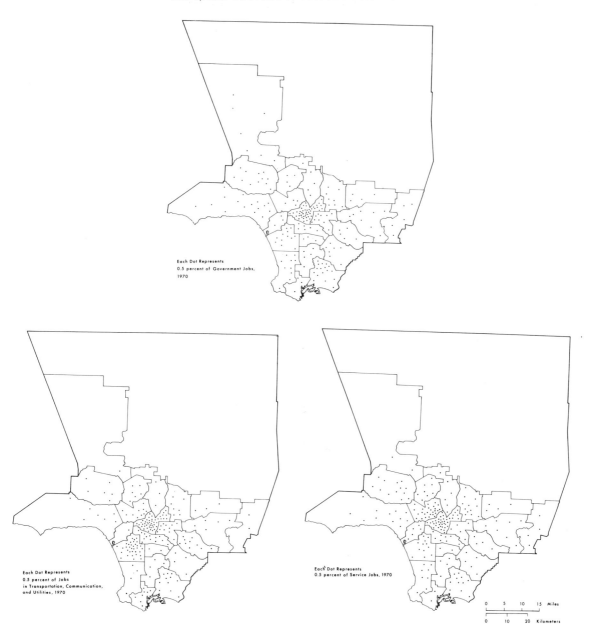

Figure 24. The distribution of government, transportation, and service employment, 1970.

of the urban area, it still most decidedly converges on central Los Angeles. If wholesalers are to maximize accessibility to their many suppliers and to the thousands of retail outlets in the area then the best location is at the center of the transport network. However, wholesalers need space for warehousing and docking facilities, and they must have a loca-

tion which is relatively free of congestion. The downtown business district satisfies neither of these criteria. Since space is too expensive to devote to warehousing, and both congestion and city ordinance prohibit the free movement of the wholesaler's trucks in this area, the logical solution is to choose the next most accessible location not as desirable for high-

Each Dot Represents
0.5 percent of
Manufacturing Jobs, 1970

Each Dot Represents
0.5 percent of
Retailing Jobs, 1970

Figure 25. The distribution of manufacturing and retail employment, 1970.

rise office buildings and retail establishments. Over the years, as the central business district has expanded, the wholesaling industry has gradually shifted to the less expensive land just to the south and east of downtown, until the majority of the wholesaling activity is now jointly shared between three labor market areas—Central Los Angeles, East Los Angeles, and Avalon-Florence. The problem of congestion is partially solved by this shift away from the central business district, but even this area is notorious for its traffic tie-ups. In fact, location has a fourth dimension—the time dimension—and wholesalers, among others, exploit this fourth dimension as a means of solving the congestion problem. Two activities such as finance and wholesaling may both use the same limited space allocated for streets and freeways in the center of Los Angeles *if* they do not all try to use the transport network at the same time. As the stockbroker is getting ready for bed after a hard day at the office, the produce trucks are rolling into the city. By 3:00 A.M. the central city is completely transformed. The offices are dark monoliths and the loading docks of the produce markets are alive with activity.

MULTIPLE FOCI ACTIVITIES

Government, transportation-communications, and service activities all have distributions which lie somewhere between the concentrated pattern of finance or wholesaling and the dispersed pattern of retail and manufacturing activities. The composite pattern generated by these three distributions (Figure 24) is a clustered or multiple foci pattern with the central city serving as the dominant focal point.

Approximately one-fourth of all jobs in transportation-communications and utilities are located in the central area of Los Angeles. From the previous discussion of the centralizing influences of the transport network upon wholesaling activity, it is not hard to see why much of the transportation industry is located in central Los Angeles, and more specifically why it is concentrated in the wholesaling or warehouse district just to the southeast of downtown. The transportation industry does, however, have an important secondary focus in the Inglewood area, reflecting a concentration of activity in and immediately surrounding Los Angeles International Airport. Unfortunately,

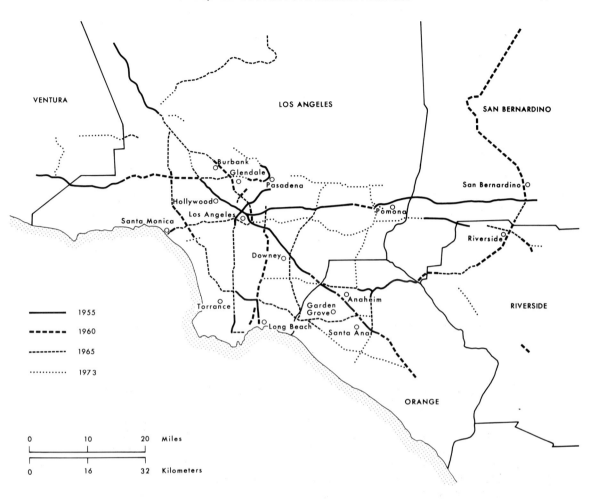

Figure 26. Development of the freeway system, 1955–1973.

air transport needs vast amounts of space. Further growth in the Inglewood area is hampered by the lack of open land in which to expand. One solution appears to be the construction of a second major airport on open land beyond the built-up portions of the Los Angeles area. If the current plan is adopted, a third focus of transportation employment would emerge at Palmdale in the distant Antelope Valley.

Employment in communications and utilities is distributed in much the same fashion as government jobs and for much the same reason. In each instance the industry or the function is dominated by a small number of very large organizations such as the Southern California Gas Company which serves most of the metropolitan region. These organizations usually have branch offices, but most of the activity is concentrated at a single location to minimize time and effort in communication between departments within the same organization. Historical precedent and the cost of moving to another location, plus a need to be accessible to the entire metropolitan area, combine to make the city center the preferred site for government offices and for the main offices of communication and utility companies. However employment in these categories is not as concentrated in the downtown area as is finance or wholesaling, primarily because a large number of employees both in government and in communications and utilities are located so as to serve the needs of a community rather than the needs of the entire metropolitan area. Thus branch offices in charge of a variety of government services are located in such diverse locations as Van Nuys, West Los Angeles, and Pomona.

A rather diverse combination of jobs, ranging from clerical to maintenance work, falls within the service class, a category that accounts for 22 percent of all jobs in the Los Angeles County region. The map of service employment could be thought of as a double exposure. It represents not one but two rather distinct distributions; one is a clustered pattern reflecting the concentration of services in and around the central business district, the other is a dispersed pattern. This distribution emphasizes the important fact that service jobs are created for two rather distinct purposes. On the one hand, the large commercial and public organizations located in or near the central business district must employ thousands of lawyers, secretaries, and clerks (not to mention janitors) to handle the details of daily operation. Without them business would come to a grinding halt. On the other hand, many other services are oriented toward the satisfaction of the needs and desires of the individual consumer. Services of this type are located in the older satellite cities such as Pasadena, Burbank, and Santa Monica as foci for government activity and are also distributed along major arterials traversing those urbanized areas which grew up with the automobile.

DISPERSED ACTIVITIES

If we put aside differences in scale, the distribution of manufacturing jobs appears to be surprisingly similar to maps of manufacturing for other large cities. Los Angeles has a garment district located where one would expect on the border of the downtown area. Most of the heavy manufacturing and the oil refineries are located beyond the warehouse district along the rail lines and the freeways to the southeast of downtown or near the habor. The availability of large tracts of land at low prices on the outskirts of the city is attractive to new manufacturing firms. In fact, one can almost determine the age of a firm or even a whole industry in Los Angeles by its distance from the center of the city. The same process is at work in the manufacturing sector of other large

cities, but few have yet attained the degree of dispersion found in Los Angeles.

The rapid rate of dispersion is due in part to the type of manufacturing which has been attracted to Los Angeles. Much of Los Angeles' early growth can be attributed to the aircraft and the motion picture industries which came to Los Angeles in their infancy. Locations near the center of town were not practical, since they required large areas of vacant land for runways or for back lots and studios. As the city grew, however, these two industries also grew. New sites had to be located still greater distances from the city center.

The dispersed nature of manufacturing in Los Angeles is also a function of the relative newness of its industrial base. Few plants are over fifty years old and their locations are consonant with the needs of today's manufacturers. The pattern of manufacturing in older cities only partially reflects current locational decisions; the remainder of the pattern is a legacy from the past. Current technology dictates the need for a single story, space-using, plant design as opposed to the vertical, space-conserving design which was suited to eighteenth and nineteenth century technology. In Los Angeles, today's space-using plants must seek locations along the radiating transport network on the fringes of the city where open land is available and relatively inexpensive.

When discussing the distribution of economic activities, one does not normally think of manufacturing and retailing as having similar distributions. Even the casual observer can see that these two activities are seldom located in juxtaposition. Ideal retail locations are those which are maximally accessible to large numbers of potential customers. Usually such locations are grouped together to form a shopping center, commercial strip, or central business district near large residential areas. Manufacturing firms would never seek locations with these attributes. Although these two activities appear to be almost antithetical in their locational requirements, the fact still remains that at the level of aggregation shown in Figure 27 the distribution of retail jobs is with few exceptions very similar to the distribution of manufacturing jobs. In both cases, the central Los Angeles area has ceased to be the undisputed focal point of economic activity. Almost every labor market in the Los Angeles area is an important source of employment in both

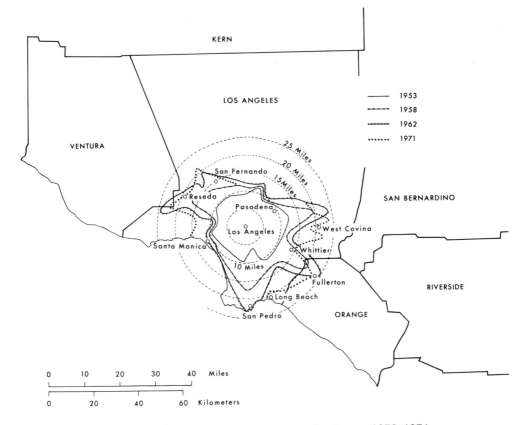

Figure 27. Changes in the thirty minute isochrone, 1953-1971.

categories. The only notable exceptions are the heavily industrialized areas to the southeast of the city center and the Hollywood-Beverly Hills area to the northwest of the central city. In the first area population density is low and incomes are even lower; consequently retail activity is underrepresented in the area, whereas manufacturing makes a very strong showing. The reverse is true of the second area, which has a very active retail and service sector while manufacturing is discouraged—with the exception of the movie industry, which is glamorous and not obnoxious—both by zoning ordinance and by high land values.

Turning exclusively now to a discussion of retail activity, the distribution of employment, aside from the exceptions mentioned above, is almost identical to the distribution of population in the metropolitan area. Since the population density in many areas of Los Angeles is not particularly high, retail activity must be widely dispersed. On the one hand, specific

retail stores must be near other complementary stores to minimize the length of multipurpose trips made by the consumer. Retailers have found two answers to this dual problem—a linear answer and a nodal answer; or, in other words, the commercial strip and the shopping center. The solutions are far from being unique to Los Angeles. In fact, the map of retail employment for Los Angeles is very much like a map of retail employment for Denver or Detroit or Dallas. The same major strips and minor nodes occur in all these cities. It may be that Los Angeles is only a somewhat more extreme case of a general pattern occurring in every metropolitan area. Increasing suburbanization is a trait common to all large cities. It would appear that this force inevitably leads to the increased dispersion of retail activity and its coalescence into commercial strips and shopping centers in the newly developed suburban areas.

Movement in the Metropolis

A wide variety of foreign and customized automobiles moving down a crowded four lane freeway is the clear national image of Angelenos and their means of movement. In fact, rapid accessibility to the varied locations of the metropolis is part of the lifestyle of southern California. In the eyes of some observers this phenomenon has been considered unique. To others it is the wave of the future, and to many it is a sad commentary on urban life in the twentieth century. Actually, the presence of a freeway system in Los Angeles is a logical development; travel by automobile in American cities may have become a national rather than local phenomenon, and as a system of movement compared to others it has both assets and liabilities. Finally, the area is currently making some plans toward a traditional mass transit system.

As we have seen, the Los Angeles region, during its twentieth century growth period, was widespread, with irregularly spaced centers covering hundreds of square miles. Although tied together loosely with an extensive streetcar and interurban system, this situation did not prevent automobiles from becoming popular very early. The climate made year round operation possible even in the days of open, heaterless automobiles, when cars in the eastern cities were left on blocks in garages for many winter months. As early as 1915, although Los Angeles county had only 750,000 inhabitants, its 55,217 automobiles made it the nation's leading county in automobile ownership. Cars were so numerous in the region that in 1920 the city council passed a no parking ordinance

for the downtown streets. The *Los Angeles Times* in opposing the ordinance headlined: "Business Can't Do Without Them." Caravans of cars protested the law, which was soon repealed. Perhaps to assert their new powers, owners of automobiles founded the Southern California Automobile Club in 1927. And in 1925 the first building was built facing the rear, with its major entrance leading from the parking lot.

So it was not surprising, with the automobile already present in record numbers during the period the area was growing to metropolitan size, that a system of grade-separated parkways was planned to continue the region's mobility. Plans for a parkway system seem to have come out of the first traffic survey in 1934. However, the area's first freeway—the Arroyo Seco Parkway, a six mile "miracle boulevard" designed to carry an astounding 27,000 cars a day—was not dedicated until the last day of 1940. It connected, as had the first intercity streetcar line, the downtown center with Pasadena. World War II dictated a postponement of the program but by the early 1950s a number of freeways were radiating from a six level downtown interchange toward Hollywood, San Bernardino, Santa Ana, and the harbor. They were rapidly extended and others were added (Figure 26). Later circumferential segments were built so that all regional traffic did not have to use the downtown focus to move about the area, and a true freeway *system* evolved.

Today the Los Angeles region has within it some twenty-three freeways or parts of freeways, comprising some 620 miles and built at a cost of about $3 billion. There are some four million automobiles in Los Angeles and Orange County, approximately one for every 2.2 persons. Moreover, from 1940 to 1970 the number of automobiles increased faster than the rate of population growth. Specifically, in this period, the number of automobiles increased 225 percent, while the population of Los Angeles county increased by only 154 percent.

ASSETS OF THE AUTOMOBILES

If an element of the goal of the good life in southern California is freedom of movement over a large area, it can be argued that the automobile and the freeway achieve this for much of the time. As Banham puts it: "[t]he private car and the public freeway together provide an ideal ... version of democratic urban transportation: door to door movement, on demand, at high average speeds over a very large area."

It is perhaps overstating the case to go further, as Banham does, and characterize the freeway system as a fourth ecology, "Autopia," a single comprehensible place, a complete way of life. And one should not take seriously literature such as John Didion's *Play It As It Lays,* in which the principal character drives the freeways daily for hours with no destination, attuned to their currents as a riverman is to those of a river, and dreaming at night of the signs passing overhead, all as a kind of perverse therapy. However, one should recognize that freeways are highly visible landscape features, with their own architectural importance. Further, it can be asserted that with a few exceptions the freeway system works surprisingly well and makes much of the 1,200 square mile Los Angeles basin accessible to the automobile driver.

ACCESSIBILITY IN LOS ANGELES

One measure of accessibility is the distance one can go from a point in a given period of time. In the 1953–1962 period in the Los Angeles area, the thirty minute isochrone (the distance from the center one could reach in that time) moved regularly outward, roughly following new freeway construction and highway improvement (Figure 27). Over the nine year period the land area within the thirty minute travel zone from the Los Angeles civic center

increased from 261 to 705 square miles, an increase of approximately 175 percent. However, the addition of the 1971 isochrone shows little increase in the area reachable in thirty minutes and some parts of the city actually experienced a slight decrease in accessibility. This may be due to the fact that by the latter decade the freeways radiating out from the center were basically complete. Additions to the system were generally suburban or circumferential and fed cars into the radial routes without adding further spokes. But, in general, the change in the transportation system has benefited a large number of people and increased the freedom and mobility to which we have already referred and, with the establishment in the sixties of a more gridlike freeway system, movement across the metropolitan area has improved.

A second measure of accessibility or freedom of movement has to do with distance from home to workplace. How far from work is it feasible to live? Apparently it is possible to have a home considerably farther from work in Los Angeles than in the older eastern cities. Mean commuting distances are smaller for New York and Philadelphia, for example, and whereas about 15 percent of New York commuters travel distances of about five miles, only 5 percent of the Los Angeles commuters travel this minimal distance (Figure 28). Stratified by income, distances between home and work are greater at all income levels in Los Angeles as compared to New York. In both cases, the distances between home and work increase with increasing income. In both metropolitan areas the wealthy trade longer commuting for the advantages of suburban living. Residents with incomes over $15,000 in New York traveled approximately 7.7 miles to work while in Los Angeles the same group traveled 10.5 miles. On the other hand, in both areas residents with incomes of about $2,000 traveled five miles or less.

Two affluent and two low income districts yield more specific details on home and workplace separation. The residents of Brentwood and Beverly Crest (affluent) traveled much greater average distances than did the residents of Watts and Boyle Heights. Not only did they travel greater distances, they traveled to a more widely varying set of locations within the city. Comments on the modes of accessibility available in the two regions are also re-

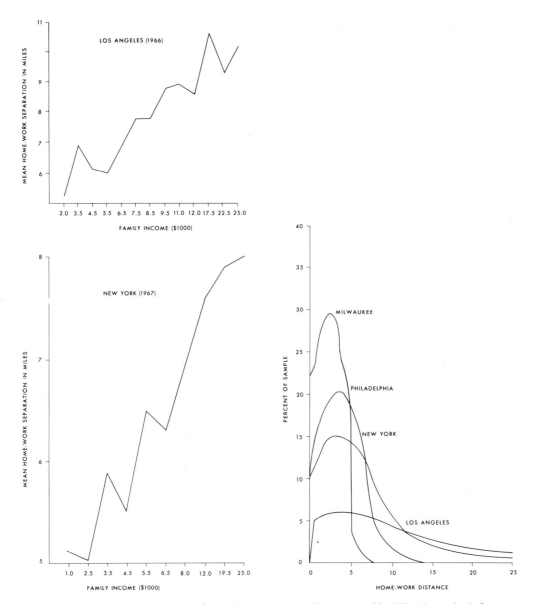

Figure 28. Distance traveled to work in selected metropolitan areas. Modified from A. J. Catanese, "Home and Workplace Separation in Four Urban Regions," *Journal of the American Institute of Planners* 37 (1971): 331–37.

vealing. In Beverly Crest 94 percent of the households have an automobile and 62 percent have two or more. The figures for Brentwood are 90 percent and 51 percent respectively. On the other hand, only 58 percent of the households in Watts have automobiles, as do 60 percent of the households in Boyle Heights. The proportions with two more autos are only

2.6 percent and 11.7 percent respectively. This means that at least four out of ten of the families in these low income areas must depend on the local bus line for transportation to work or for any movement. While transit resources seem to be allocated to areas with low rates of auto ownership, they often are not routed to areas of possible employment, and many of the desired destinations can be reached only circuitously and after a lengthy, time-consuming ride.

Despite these comments, Los Angeles seems to be similar to if not totally like New York and the parallels of income and distance between workplace and home are striking. The mild climate and vast range of used automobiles somewhat mitigate what could be particularly discriminating aspects of accessibility in Los Angeles.

While accessibility and long distance commuting seem to be characteristic of the Los Angeles area, the concept of neighborhood mentioned earlier still operates. For many purposes residents use only a small portion of the metropolitan area for their common daily activities. In the Mar Vista studies described earlier, for many activities—such as the location of friends, clubs, community organizations, and recreational activities—the neighborhood is the base. Sixty-three percent of the wives'

activities occurred within five miles of the home (although the husbands' activity patterns, more specifically tied to their commuting patterns, have a wider range). Seventy-one percent of the wives' friends live within five miles, and even for the husband 60 percent of his friends are from the same nearby area (Figure 29).

Although the Los Angeles freeway system has given its residents a great deal of accessibility necessary for the good life, they have not been an unmitigated success. They are of little use, in the first place, to that proportion of the population that, because they are too young, too old, or too poor, have no access to an automobile. Any system based on the automobile is inefficient in the use of energy and constitutes a major source of pollution. It can also be argued that the freeways have not fully attained the objectives of their original proponents. These included reducing traffic on surface streets, reducing

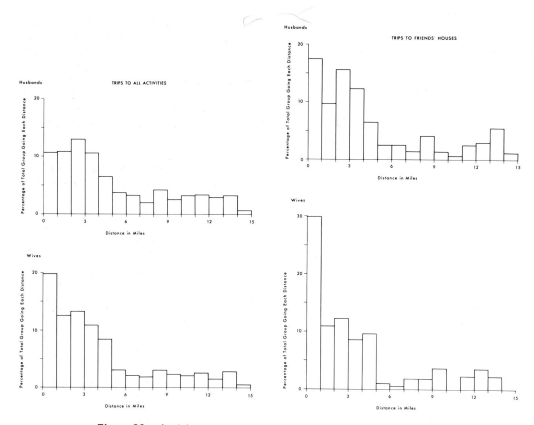

Figure 29. Activity patterns for a sample of Mar Vista residents.

driving time from point to point, and reducing the automobile accident and fatality rates.

As of today the goal of congestion-free circulation has not been achieved. In part this is related to the sequence of events following the construction of a freeway. Traffic in parallel streets declines considerably, but traffic on intersecting streets increases a great deal. As years pass, traffic on the parallel streets slowly builds up to its prefreeway level. W.A. McDaniel concludes: "In the long run, all major facilities in the vicinity (of the two freeways tested) are found to accommodate constantly increasing demands." Further, the completion of a freeway seems to induce new traffic from two sources—trips that were made by other modes, such as a bus, and trips that were not made at all. A Los Angeles City traffic study indicates that 29 percent of the traffic on the Santa Monica Freeway was induced traffic. Added to this, in the long run, will be trips from new land developments encouraged by the freeway.

Again, some recent data indicate that peak hour travel time on selected freeways has been increasing. Average peak driving time on the five freeways has increased from two to three times in less than a decade (Table 6).

Table 6. Peak Hour Travel Times on Selected Los Angeles Freeways

Route	*Average Peak Hour Trip Time in Minutes*	
	1956-1958:	*1965:*
Harbor Freeway, Civic Center to Santa Barbara Avenue	5:50	10:00
Hollywood Freeway, Civic Center to Hollywood and Vine	7:35	25:00
Pasadena Freeway, Civic Center to Glenarm	10:30	25:00
San Bernardino Freeway, Civic Center to Rosemead	12:51	30:00
Santa Ana Freeway, Civic Center to Norwalk Boulevard	16:40	40:00

Sources: Paul McElhiney, "Evaluation of Freeway Performance in Los Angeles," *Traffic Quarterly* 14 (1960): 305, and Automobile Club of Southern California, *1965 Los Angeles Metropolitan Travel Time Study* (Los Angeles, 1966).

Finally, if one measures perso〔 nual motor vehicle fatality rate persons, risk is still considerably Los Angeles area than in citie modes of travel (Table 7). It i: fatality rate in the Los Angeles area is low per million vehicle miles driven and that freeways are safer than ordinary streets. However, as McDaniel points out, this advantage has been "entirely negated because Angelenos have deemed it desirable or necessary to drive many more miles than their counterparts in other cities."

IS LOS ANGELES A UNIQUELY AUTOMOBILE CITY?

Despite the descriptions of freeways and accessibility which we have presented to this point, is there justification for the assertion that Los Angeles is unique? Comparative evidence is fragmentary but it is obvious that at least in terms of automobile ownership Los Angeles is no longer the most automobile-oriented SMSA. Both Seattle and Denver have more automobiles per household than Los Angeles, and Detroit, Cleveland, and San Francisco-Oakland all have ratios which are not especially dissimilar (Table 8). Apart from the New York region, Boston, and Philadelphia, the measure of persons per automobile is almost the same for all United States metropolitan areas. But, possibly more important, the

Table 7. Comparison of Motor Vehicle Fatality Rates (fatalities per 100,000 persons)

	Motor Vehicle Fatality Rate (Including Vehicle-Related Pedestrian Fatalities)			
Year	*New York*	*Phila-delphia*	*Chicago*	*Los Angeles*
1942	10.8	12.7	13.7	21.3
1945	9.6	9.1	13.9	27.9
1947	9.6	10.2	15.0	21.8
1948	7.5	7.3	12.8	15.5
1951	7.0	8.0	11.5	13.6
1954	7.5	8.9	10.9	14.8
1957	8.1	8.2	8.5	17.8
1960	7.6	8.5	7.6	15.7
1963	8.5	8.7	8.2	13.6
1966	7.4	9.3	9.0	16.2
1969	10.7	10.0	9.4	17.2

Sources: National Safety Council, *Accident Facts* (Chicago, published annually).

Table 8. Ratio of Autos Owned to Households for Selected Large SMSAs, 1960 and 1970 Averages

	Ratio, Autos to Households	
SMSA	*1960*	*1970*
Boston	0.91	1.07
New York	0.64	0.75
Philadelphia	0.91	1.13
Pittsburgh	0.93	1.11
Chicago	0.89	1.06
Detroit	1.11	1.32
Cleveland	1.05	1.26
Denver	1.23	1.46
St. Louis	0.94	1.21
Minneapolis-St. Paul	1.10	1.31
Dallas	1.19	1.44
Los Angeles-Long Beach	1.21	1.33
San Francisco-Oakland	1.05	1.22
Seattle	1.12	1.36

Sources: U.S. Bureau of the Census, U.S. Census of Housing 1970, *Detailed Housing Characteristics– U.S. Summary*, HC(1)B1, Table 40; and U.S. Census of Housing 1960, *States and Small Areas–U.S. Summary*, HC(1) no. 1, Table 19.

measure of households without a car shows that both Detroit and Minneapolis have a lower percentage of families without automobiles than Los Angeles. As the suburbs have grown around all metropolitan areas, new shopping centers and other services have followed. Increasingly, suburban residents find employment in the suburbs. But to move around the suburbs—whether in Detroit, Chicago, or Los Angeles—it is necessary to have wheels. The new land use pattern of the metropolitan suburban locations has made it more or less imperative to have one car and, until the energy crisis, preferably two cars. While the automobile has had its most visual impact in Los Angeles, many observers would be hard put, if placed blindfolded in a suburban sector of a large American metropolitan area, to immediately identify the precise metropolitan area they were observing.

But the impact is not just in automobile ownership, the impact of the automobile can best be seen in the increased construction of freeways. We have already noted the extent of development in Los Angeles. But there are 900 miles of expressway in New York, 400 miles in Chicago, and over 200 miles of freeway in Detroit. The impact is also seen in the pervasive use of the automobile as the major means of transportation. The proportion of work trips by automobile ranges between 75 percent in the central city and 86 percent in the suburbs in Los Angeles. In Detroit the percentages are 68 and 86, and for Chicago the range is from 63 to 76 percent (Table 9). Denver, Oklahoma City, and Forth Worth are all directly comparable and even in the suburban areas of eastern cities the percent of travel by the automobile ranges between 65 and 78 percent. Public transport accounted for an average of only 25 percent of the work trips in the thirty largest SMSAs. The evidence for a unique Los Angeles is not particularly striking; rather, the evidence points up the pervasiveness of the automobile in all United States metropolitan areas.

And finally, not only is the Los Angeles condition with regard to automobile movement becoming commonplace in newer cities

Table 9. The Journey to Work by Mode of Travel

	Number of Workers	*Percentage Using Each Mode*			
Destination		*Auto*	*Bus*	*Walked*	*Other*
Central Los Angeles					
Zone I	49,771	38	37	20	5
Zone II	146,063	59	30	7	4
Zone III	296,737	73	17	5	5
West Los Angeles	133,563	84	6	5	5
South Los Angeles	41,147	80	5	7	8
San Fernando Valley	257,764	90	2	3	5
All Workers	925,045	76	14	6	4

Source: Circulation Element for the Los Angeles City General Plan, Staff Working Paper, Los Angeles, Department of City Planning, 1970.

like Denver and Dallas, but within the next few decades the Los Angeles region might move toward the New York-Philadelphia pattern with the beginning of a mass rapid transit system. With freeway construction stalled, many people seem agreed that an additional means of movement is necessary. A proposal for an eighty-eight mile "subway," "fixed rail," "backbone" network was defeated in 1968, when only about 45 percent of the voters responded favorably. Even so, the bond issue received over one million yes votes—in spite of the additional taxes it would entail. Currently, another proposal of the same sort is being prepared for voter approval in a psychological climate much less committed to the automobile and freeway.

Conclusion

Beebe's vigorous comment (cited in W.W. Robinson) may be extreme, but a general theme of disenchantment is characteristic of much of the literature on Los Angeles. This feeling seems particularly common in the writing produced in the period between the two World Wars, but earlier examples exist and some persists today. Sometimes the basis for disapproval is easily understandable; in other instances the causes are obscure, but the reaction generally seems to have its roots in the elements of uniqueness found by the writers in the people and in the city itself.

It is easy, for example, to explain Beebe's feelings. One would hardly expect a chronicler and arbiter of society, a habitué of the aging parlors of Boston and the grand drawing rooms of New York, to find much that was pleasing in Los Angeles. Here the social scene was severely limited, if not nonexistent. The really old families were forgotten, remembered only in street names, while the newly rich and powerful were just getting established. What real society existed was apt to be found in suburban Pasadena, or more likely in distant Santa Barbara. While a local resident could understand how the establishment of "Pickfair" by Mary Pickford and Douglas Fairbanks would give an upper class tone to Beverly Hills that would endure for decades, Beebe would be the last to confuse celebrity with aristocracy.

Readily comprehensible, too, is the literature hostile to the Los Angeles milieu that poured from the typewriters of numerous professional writers who were brought to the area to work in the movie industry. Transported from their familiar haunts in London or New York to, say, the pool-fringed, rococo bungalows of the Garden of Allah Hotel, and from the creativity of free-lance writing to the highly paid but captive chore of turning out popular film scripts, their reactions were predictably negative. The film industry itself, the *nouveaux riches* entrepreneurs who ran it, and the glittery, artificial environment of "Hollywood" and its many shattered dreams had—and has—much that invited satire. Books such as Nathaniel West's *The Day of the Locust* and Budd Schulberg's *What Makes Sammy Run?* were the natural result.

But the Los Angeles literature of disenchantment is not limited to the shafts of socialites and the satires of film writers. More objective observers also went away unsatisfied and disappointed. Los Angeles, particularly in the early decades of this century, was different in its population mix, urban accouterments, and perhaps even in its intellectual atmosphere. It is probable that it was these differences that many visitors found disturbing. As we have seen, Los Angeles generally missed the great influx of European immigrants that gave most eastern cities their character early in this century. Whether the typical ethnic enclave was as pleasant a place to live in as its was exciting to observe is not the point. These areas were colorful spots, provided a dynamic and varied street life, and were a vital part of the "normal" urban scene. And their residents, who had journeyed to America with empty pockets seeking "freedom," were easier to admire than midwesterners who had come to Los Angeles with a financial "nest egg" and wanting only to be warm. Then too, there was something not quite urban about a city that had no subways or elevated trains, but instead depended on the streetcar or interurban for mass transit. Interurbans, after all, in the rest of America, were the transportation of the countryside, not of the city. Similarly, the automobile, popular so early in Los Angeles, might be used by Aunt Sadie on the farm to go to town, but not by Uncle Harry to commute to his urban office.

But Los Angeles not only lacked some of the phenomena which characterized eastern cities, it was also responsible for creating some unique features of its own. For example, where else would a cemetery prove to be the biggest tourist attraction for more than three decades? Actually it wasn't called a cemetery; rather, Forest Lawn Memorial Park. It didn't even look like a cemetery. It had no granite tombstones, only bronze markers, almost invisible among the landscaped, statue-studded, tree-shaded acres. And the chapels within it—The Little Church of the Flowers, The Wee Kirk of the Heather—were more often used for weddings than for funerals. To the surprise of few, it became a favorite target of derision—for example, Evelyn Waugh's *The Loved Ones*. But also, to the consternation of many, it revolutionized mortuary practice and cemetery development around the country.

Perhaps some of the expressed dissatisfaction was simply a reaction to unfulfilled expectations, for satisfaction is not a stable thing, but advances along with promises, hopes, and dreams. And perhaps the American dream of California—a new start, a better life, increasing happiness—was, for many, an unrealistic and unattainable goal, in Los Angeles or anywhere. Not everyone made his fortune by buying residential lots in Westwood. Not every girl who sipped a cherry coke in Schwab's Drugstore became a movie star. Not everyone

who was looking for even an ordinary job found a satisfactory way to make a living.

Finally, of course, it is the natural environment that provides the greatest contrast for the newly arrived easterner, and many found the change not entirely pleasing. "I miss a climate without four distinct seasons," was a common reaction. And at Christmas time, shouldn't we "go dashing through the snow?" Summer rains are normal, aren't they? And why should the hills have a tawny purple look instead of the usual green?

"LOS ANGELES—IT'S TURNING OUT TO BE THE MOST AMERICAN OF ALL U.S. CITIES."—HAMILTON BASSO HOLIDAY, JANUARY 1950

It seems evident that Los Angeles, particularly in the early decades of this century, if not unique, was at least somewhat different from most American cities. Its population mix was different, its housing patterns were different, its urban transportation was different, and even much of its culture seemed not entirely familiar. It is also clear than in recent decades many of these differences have tended to disappear.

Basso's characterization appears more accurate today than when he made it twenty-five years ago. He visualized Los Angeles becoming the "most American city" because it was the "melting pot" of migrants from all over the country. Further, he felt its faults and virtues were "simply our national character writ large." From the latter notion it could be implied that these same national characteristics were also operating in all American cities, Perhaps Basso's comments can be viewed as recognizing that a dual process was at work. Los Angeles was becoming like other cities and other cities would become more like Los Angeles.

Actually, even now, this process is not complete. However, the downtown of Los Angeles looks more like other downtowns. Densities have increased in the inner areas of Los Angeles and at the same time the single family ranch house has become common in all American cities. Los Angeles may have pioneered in the extensive use of the automobile, but it is now ubiquitous in all but the oldest of eastern cities.

But similarities comprise more than tall buildings, population densities, and automobile ownership. And in some of these nonmaterial qualities of "urbanness"—intellectual and artistic development, for example—Los Angeles has been a follower rather than a leader. The area's midwestern Protestant flavor has only gradually been ameliorated and transformed into a more mature and urbane society. Numerous factors have been involved—the passage of time, the increase in wealth of a proportion of the population, the arrival of substantial Jewish population, the increase of the Mexican-Americans and blacks, the influx of Ph.D.s and engineers to man the area's postwar "think tanks," and so on.

However, according to Christopher Rand, much of the change must be related to the influx of the exiled artists and intellectuals who began to arrive with the development of troubles in Europe after World War I. The refugees were attracted by the climate, by the movie industry, and, as time went on, by the presence of other exiles. Sound was added to the movies in the 1930s, with new demands for orchestras. Good musicians arriving in New York could continue right on out to Los Angeles and find work in these orchestras. As a result, Los Angeles became a music center second only to New York and ahead of it in some respects. The exiles also contributed authors and other artists and professionals. Several of their number—including Ernest Simmel and Otto Fenichel—founded the profession of psychoanalysis in the city. Others became book dealers, art dealers, and art restorers. Their zeal for self-improvement encouraged UCLA to develop what is reputed to be the best university extension service in the country. And the Los Angeles Public Library, with its many branches, became the largest circulating library in the Western world.

Recently, other symbols of increased intellectual and cultural activity have arisen. Included would be the "Music Center for the Performing Arts"—a three theatre complex in the Civic center (the home of the Los Angeles Philharmonic Orchestra, the Los Angeles County Museum of Art on Wilshire Boulevard, and, recently, the Getty Museum in the Pacific Palisades, as well as a rash of legitimate theaters. These complement the much earlier Huntington Library and Art Gallery in Pasadena and the outdoor Hollywood Bowl and Greek Theater. The universities —California Institute of Technology, University of California, and the more recently distinguished UCLA, and the numerous branches of the California State University—have also added to the intellectual and cultural base of the region.

And, occasionally, some of the elements of earlier differences in Los Angeles that remain prove to be assets rather than liabilities. Many neighborhoods of older, single family houses still stand near the center of the city, and this includes large sections of the black ghetto and Mexican-American barrio. Although poverty is rampant and unemployment is unconscionably high among the residents of those areas, some of the most degrading aspects of urban slums associated with the solid blocks of multistory buildings characteristic of eastern cities are not present. Similarly, the earlier absence of large ethnic minorities has enabled the region to escape the more virulent of the ethnic jealousies often so difficult to resolve in some American cities. One can not ignore the rivalry and suspicion between some elements of the black and Mexican-American communities who are often competing for the same unskilled jobs. But as a hopeful symbol for the future, the city of Los Angeles elected a black mayor, Tom Bradley, in 1973 (after a near miss four years earlier) with a minimum of rancor and controversy.

EDEN IN JEOPARDY. . . . THE SOUTHERN CALIFORNIA EXPERIENCE—RICHARD G. LILLARD

Ironically, and perhaps significantly, as the Los Angeles area has become more "normal" in many of its urban aspects, and as its culture has become more mature (and perhaps more acceptable to its critics), the region has lost its formerly appealing popular image. Owning an orange grove, working in Hollywood, or living in a California Bungalow are no longer the main goals of most migratory Americans. These images of Los Angeles have largely passed, and in the minds of the present generation the area conjures up only smog, crowded freeways, despoiled nature, and sprawling bigness in general.

The automobile seemed the ideal vehicle to enable man to move freely and independently over southern California's expansive space and to fully enjoy the inviting outdoors with its bright sunshine, warm temperatures, and light winds. But, as we have seen, its exhaust fumes are particularly unsuited for just such an atmosphere. And, although smog is far from omnipresent and all pervasive, at times and in places it is not only a nuisance for the good life but a menace to good health. The area's attempts to control air pollution have been vigorous, its research has been pioneering, its political organization imaginative, and its air pollution laws and standards have been models for the rest of the nation. Yet three decades of effort have succeeded only in slowing the increase of pollution and altering its composition. Real progress seems to await the development of a pollution-free automobile engine, an achievement beyond the power of the region to effect.

Air pollution aside, the dependence of the region on automobiles and freeways as a means of transportation poses real problems, although not because the combination does not provide fast and comfortable transportation, at most times and in most places. (And if you are going to have automobiles you must have freeways, as anyone who has tried to move in an automobile in a city without freeways—London, for example—can attest.) The problem, rather, is that the automobile, on a freeway or not, is inherently inefficient in its use of resources, is by its nature unsafe, and is forever fated to be unavailable to large segments of the population that should not be ignored—the young, the old, the poor, and those with an inclination not to drive.

A greatly improved mass rapid transit system for the region, with at least some electrified, fixed rail, grade-separated elements, seems essential. A proposal for such a system has been prepared by the Rapid Transit District, financed through a sales tax increase, and will be submitted to the voters in November 1974. Even if approved, however, the only immediate effect would be an expanded bus system; the more sophisticated rapid transit portions are at least a decade away.

Even though the nation's image of southern California in the 1970s is not entirely in harmony with reality, it cannot be denied that much of the earlier, almost bucolic quality of the area has been forever lost. Subdivisions have replaced the orange groves of the San Gabriel Valley, Wilshire Boulevard no longer bisects bean fields but is bordered by offices and shops, and the poppies are gone from the populated slopes of Altadena. The passing of these natural and agricultural landscapes is mourned by many, particularly by those who knew them. Yet one must not fall into the trap of earlier self-centered observers. Even in a period of renewed appreciation of nature, it is not certain that residents would opt en masse for the "good life," a hillside of flowers may not always seem more desirable than access to a professional sports team, bean fields along a highway may be less important than a delicatessen at the corner, an orange grove may not be nearly as essential as a golf course.

But in spite of massive urban development, a surprising number of the area's natural assets for the good life are still present. Climates change only imperceptibly, the oceans do not disappear, and the earth abides. For the American seeking the good life, the summer air is still dry, the nights remain cool, the winters continue to be balmy—and the resident is beckoned out-of-doors almost as before. The waves break on a hundred miles of sandy beach as they always have; the inviting ocean still stretches onward toward the setting sun. The mountains yet intrude into the urbanized city, visible and accessible to nearly every one. It is a truly disadvantaged or unimaginative youth who cannot occasionally find his way to a strip of beach or a secluded mountain path.

Even so, the preservation of these natural qualities for future generations is problematical. Although new steps are taken annually to reduce air pollution, much more drastic measures are clearly needed, including an imaginative program of mass rapid transit. The petroleum and automobile industries are among the country's most powerful; mass transit remains wildly expensive and an uncertain experiment in the minds of a somewhat skeptical public. Yet it seems improbable that this crime against nature will be allowed to continue indefinitely. Additional privately owned shoreline is gradually being added to the already extensive system of public beaches. However, the continental shelf of the entire region is a potentially productive petroleum resource with all of the dangers for beach contamination that such activity entails. Although some areas of the mountains have been converted to urban uses, many slopes are steep and isolated and as a result much of the mountain lands remains undeveloped. However, portions are being acquired for public use by local, state, and national agencies. That the pace is maddeningly slow reflects not so much local desire as the financial difficulties of local agencies and the strange priorities of administrations in Sacramento and Washington.

Perhaps for the first time, the perils of massive growth are apparent to the region's residents and the slogan that bigger is necessarily better would get few takers today. Southern Californians, if a January 1970 opinion survey is valid, recognize population growth as a cause of environmental problems, believe policies to restrict further population increases to be justified, and disapprove actions that are thought to encourage inmigration. Further, the same survey indicates that the family size most desired by southern Californians is lower than that of the nation as a whole. Reflecting the new mood, current planning proposals for the city of Los Angeles call for a rollback in zoning to reduce residential capacity of the city through changes in both single family and multiple-zoned areas and other reductions in the intensity of potential new development. So far, however, these last measures have been more token than significant.

In reality, in parts of the region at least, the lengthy era of growth seems to have come to an end. The city of Los Angeles, belatedly following the pattern of other large cities, has been losing population since 1970. And in 1973, for the first time in 123 years, Los Angeles County lost population. However, the outlying counties—Ventura, Orange, Riverside, and San Bernardino—continue to grow, although at a slower pace. In any event, southern California seems to be entering a somewhat different era of development and one that has the clear approval of its residents. For at least fifty years the area has suffered national derision for its boosterism. One wonders if it would now win universal acclaim by adopting for its motto the Cotter's Prayer:

We thank thee Lord, that by Thy grace
Thou hast led us to this lovely place
And now, dear Lord, we humbly pray
Thou will all others keep away.

Bibliography

Air Pollution Control District, County of Los Angeles. *Profile of Air Pollution Control.* Los Angeles, 1971.

Automobile Club of Southern California. *Los Angeles Metropolitan Peak Hour Driving Study.* Los Angeles, June 1957.

——. *Los Angeles Metropolitan Peak Hour Driving Study.* Los Angeles, June 1960.

——. *Peak Hour Driving Study Metropolitan Los Angeles.* Los Angeles, May 1962.

Automobile Club of Southern California and Los Angeles Junior Chamber of Commerce. *1965 Los Angeles Metropolitan Travel Time Study.* Los Angeles, July 1966.

Bailey, Harry P. *The Climate of Southern California.* California Natural History Guides, no. 17. Berkeley: University of California Press 1966.

Banham, Reyner. *Los Angeles, The Architecture of the Four Ecologies.* New York: Harper and Row, 1971.

Basso, Ham. Hon. "Los Angeles", *Holiday* 7, 1, (January 1950): 26–47.

Behar, Joseph V. "Simulation Model of Air Pollution Photo Chemistry." *Project Clean Air,* University of California Research Report, Vol. 4, 1970.

Bell, Horace. *Reminiscences of a Ranger or Early Times in Southern California.* Los Angeles: Yarnell, Coystile & Mathes, 1881.

Bigger, Richard. *Flood Control in Metropolitan Los Angeles.* Berkeley: University of California Publications in Political Science, vol. 6, 1959.

Bigger, Richard, and J.D. Kitchen. *How the Cities Grew.* Los Angeles: The Haynes Foundation, 1952.

Bond, J. Max. "The Negro in Los Angeles." University of Southern California Doctoral Dissertation, 1936. Reprinted by R & E Research Associates, San Francisco, 1972.

Camarillo, Alberto M. "Chicano Urban History: A Study of Compton's Barrio, 1936–1970. *Aztlan* 2, 2 (1971): 79–106.

Catanese, Anthony J. "Home and Workplace Separation in Four Urban Regions." *Journal of the American Institute of Planners* 37 (1971): 331–37.

City of Los Angeles, Community Analysis Bureau. *An Analysis of the Blighted Communities of Los Angeles.* Los Angeles, 1973.

——. *The State of the City 1972.* Vol. 1. Los Angeles, 1973.

City of Los Angeles, Department of City Planning. *Preliminary Citywide Plan, Los Angeles.* Staff Report, June 1970. Los Angeles, 1970.

——. *The Visual Environment of Los Angeles.* Los Angeles, 1971.

Clark, W.A.V. and Cadwallader, Martin. "Residential Preferences: An Alternate View of Intraurban Space." *Environment and Planning* 5 (1973): 693–703.

Committee for Central City Planning, Inc. *Central City Los Angeles, 1972/1990, Preliminary General Development Plan.* Los Angeles, 1972.

County of Los Angeles Earthquake Commission. *Report of the Los Angeles County Earthquake Commission, San Fernando Earthquake, February 9, 1971.* Los Angeles, 1971.

County of Los Angeles Regional Planning Commission. *Land Use Survey 1939.* Los Angeles, 1940.

——. *Environmental Development Guide, Preliminary Summary Draft.* Los Angeles, April 1970.

——. *Environmental Development Guide.* Los Angeles, 1971.

——. *Los Angeles County Preliminary Housing Element.* Los Angeles, 1972.

Crouch, Winston W., and Beatrice Dinerman. *Southern California Metropolis: A Study in Development of Government for a Metropolitan Area.* Berkeley: University of California Press, 1964.

De Graaf, Lawrence B. "The City of Black Angels: Emergence of the Los Angeles Ghetto, 1890-1930." *Pacific Historical Review* 39, 1 (February 1970): 323-52.

Didion, Joan. *Play It As It Lays.* New York: Farrar Straus, 1970.

Eliot, Clarks W. and Griffin, Donald F. "Waterlines . . . Key to Development of Metropolitan Los Angeles." Los Angeles: Haynes Foundation, 1946.

Everitt, John. Community and Propinquity: Questions on the Structure of and Behavior Within an Urban Area. Ph.D. Dissertation, Department of Geography, University of California, Los Angeles, 1972.

Fogelson, Robert M. *The Fragmented Metropolis–Los Angeles, 1850-1930.* Cambridge, Mass.: Harvard University Press, 1967.

Foley, Donald L., and others. *Characteristics of Metropolitan Growth in California, Volume 1.* Berkeley: University of California, Institute of Urban and Regional Development, 1965.

Garst, Jonathan. "A Geographical Study of The Los Angeles Region of Southern California." Ph.D. dissertation, University of Edinburgh, 1931.

Gordon, Roni. "Time-space Convergence and its Effect on the Los Angeles Metropolitan Area. Paper, Department of Geography, University of California, Los Angeles, 1973.

Hirsch, Werner Z., ed. *Los Angeles: Viability and Prospects for Metropolitan Leadership.* New York: Praeger, 1971.

Koltnow, Peter G. *Changes in Mobility in American Cities.* Washington, D.C.: Transportation Development Division, Highway Users Federation for Safety and Mobility, 1970.

Lillard, Richard G. *Eden in Jeopardy. . . .*

The Southern California Experience. New York: Knopf, 1966.

Ludwig Salvator, Archduke of Austria. *Eine Blume aus dem Goldenen Lande: oder, Los Angeles.* Prague: H. Mercey 1878. Translated by Marguerite E. Wilber as *Los Angeles in the Sunny Seventies, A Flower From the Golden Land.* Los Angeles: Bruce McCallister. Jake Zeitlin 1929.

Mason, William M., and John A. McKinstry. *The Japanese of Los Angeles, 1869-1902.* Los Angeles: Los Angeles County Museum of Natural History, Contribution in History, no. 1, 1969.

McElhiney, Paul. "Evaluation of Freeway Performance in Los Angeles." *Traffic Quarterly* 14 (1960): 296-312.

McWilliams, Carey. *Southern California County, An Island on the Land.* New York, Duell, Sloan & Pearce, 1946.

Nadeau, Remi A. *City Makers: The Story of Southern California's First Boom.* Los Angeles: Trans-Anglo Books 1965.

National Safety Council. *Accident Facts.* Chicago, published annually.

Newmark, Harris. *Sixty Years in Southern California, 1853-1913.* New York: Knickerbocker Press, 1916.

Nishi, Midori, and Kim, Young Il. "Recent Japanese Settlement Changes in the Los Angeles Area." *Yearbook Association of Pacific Coast Geographers* 26 (1964): 23-36.

Nordhoff, Charles. *California: for Health, Pleasure, and Residence.* New York: Harper 1875.

Ostrom, Vincent. *Water and Politics: A Study of Water Policies and Administration in the Development of Los Angeles.* Los Angeles: Haynes Foundation 1953.

Prototype State-of-the-Region for Los Angeles County. Los Angeles: School of Architecture and Urban Planning, 1973.

Rand, Christopher. *Los Angeles, The Ultimate City.* New York: Oxford University Press 1967.

Rantz, S.E. *Urban Sprawl and Flooding in Southern California.* Geological Survey Circular 601-13. Washington, 1970.

Rexford, Wilson. "The Devil Wind and Wood Shingles: The Los Angeles Conflagration of 1961." *National Fire Protection Association Quarterly,* January 1962, pp. 241-88.

Robinson, W.W. *Los Angeles, A Profile.* Norman: University of Oklahoma Press, 1968.

Shevky, Eshref, and Williams, Marilyn. *Social Areas of Los Angeles.* Berkeley: University of California Press, 1949.

Taylor, Benjamin F.. *Between The Gates.* Chicago: S.C. Griggs and Co., 1879.

Thomas, William L., Jr., ed. *Man, Time and Space in Southern California.* A special supplement to the *Annals of the Association of American Geographers* 49, 3, pt. 2 (September 1959).

Transportation Association of Southern California. *Los Angeles Regional Transportation Study, 1980 Progress Report.* n.d.

About the Authors

Howard J. Nelson is currently professor of Geography at the University of California, Los Angeles. He received his Ph.D. from the University of Chicago in 1949 and has been teaching urban geography at UCLA since that date. His research interests are the internal structure of cities, city sites, and metropolitan Los Angeles.

William A.V. Clark is currently professor of Geography at the University of California, Los Angeles. He received the Ph.D. from the University of Illinois in 1964 and taught previously at the University of Canterbury in New Zealand and at the University of Wisconsin. His research interests are focused on models of urban spatial structure and spatial behavior, and particularly on the processes of residential relocation within cities.